Moonalice Legend: Posters and Words Vol. 1

May 2007 to June 2008

First Edition, December 2008

ISBN 978-0-9793314-6-6

Creative Direction by Chris Shaw
All text written by Chubby Wombat Moonalice
Art direction and design by Whitney Parker for Rock Out Books
Project management and band photography by Jay Blakesberg

Published by Moonalice Press
www.moonaliceband.com
management@moonaliceband.com

Printed in the USA

Introduction

Every new band struggles to find a name. We had lots of ideas, but eventually settled on the name "Moonalice" because it sounded cool. What we didn't realize at the time was that we hadn't actually picked "Moonalice"; the name had chosen us.

From that moment forward, the Moonalice Legend revealed itself to us at every turn. At first, we hardly knew what to make of it, but with each gig the Legend revealed more of itself. The Legend seems to be layered like a good Spanish onion. Like a good wine, it got better with time. Here is what we have learned so far:

- The tribe has existed for millennia
- It has at least two major clans
- The society is matriarchal
- Anyone can be a tribe member
- Every member is a chief
- Like Zelig, the tribe seems to have been present at a statistically improbable number of major historical events
- Moonalice culture promotes extreme tolerance, poster art, low tones, and sharing the output of tribal agriculture

So it turns out that we are the next generation of this remarkable tribe. It's an incredible responsibility for a bunch of musicians, but we think we're up to it.

We have a message for those who express doubts about the Moonalice Legend: look it up. It's on the internet. And now it's in this book. You can't get any more real than that.

The volume in your hands is a collection of words and art from the band's first year. (A Moonalice year apparently has 13 months.) The Legend entries appear as they did following each show, with only minor edits. The originals can be found on the Moonalice website (www.moonaliceband.com). A majority of the gigs were played by Moonalice 6 (Ann, Barry, G.E., Jim, Pete, and Roger). Gigs with Jack Casady are marked (7) – for Moonalice 7 – next to the venue name. We played two gigs without Ann, both indicated by a (5) next to the venue name. Each listing includes other bands on the bill, as well as guest performers who sat in with us.

This book also includes the 84 posters created for the first year's shows. Our art director, Chris Shaw, created most of the posters in this collection. Alex Fischer, Ron Donovan, David Singer, Stanley Mouse, Chuck Sperry, and Claude Shade all made brilliant contributions, as you will see. All of the posters to date are included in this book, as is the complete Legend as we know it. Legend entries for shows after June 7, 2008 can be found on the Moonalice website in the History section.

We recommend that you enjoy this book with whatever combination of low tones and agricultural products works best for you.

Thank you for being part of the tribe!

Blue Moonalice
Chubby Wombat Moonalice
Dawnman Moonalice
Hardwood Moonalice
Jesùs H. Moonalice
Sir Sinjin Moonalice
Yggdrassil Moonalice

On the bus
June 1, 2008

Sofa Of Discontents

Posters copyright 2008 Moonalice and poster artists

Chris Shaw
pages 13, 14, 17, 19, 20, 23, 25, 32, 37, 41, 42, 45, 49, 51, 53, 54, 56, 58, 65, 66, 69, 72, 74, 77, 79, 80, 85, 86, 91, 92, 100, 104, 108, 110, 113, 120, 122, 125, 131, 132, 137, 140, 147, 153, 157, 158, 162, 166, 172, 175, 176, 179, 186, 189

Alexandra Fischer
pages 29, 46, 85, 96, 107, 116, 126, 150, 168, 187

David Singer
pages 61, 62, 70, 82, 119, 129, 145, 161, 165, 181, 184

Ron Donovan
pages 103, 114, 139, 143, 149, 154

Chuck Sperry
pages 185

Stanley Mouse
pages 188

Claude Shade
pages 183

The Back Story*

Moonalice is an ancient tribe that dates back to the beginning of time. According to Moonalice Legend, the tribe descends from Piltdown Woman, or possibly from a couple of naked, snake-charmed gardeners who liked to hang around with friendly dinosaurs. In later times, the tribe evolved into two major clans. One was agricultural, the other nomadic.

The farmers were known as hippies. They cultivated many things, but their specialty was a native American crop: hemp. Over the years, the hippies found many uses for hemp and built an advanced culture around it.

The nomadic Moonalice clans were known as bands. They wandered the continent, surviving on their wits and music. Their specialty was low tones. The clans coexisted for millennia, living in harmony (and counterpoint) with all creatures.

From time to time, the Moonalice hippies and bands would gather in pow wows that were known as gigs. A precursor to modern county fairs, these celebrations brought together the best of agriculture and music. More Woodstock than livestock, Moonalice gigs were quintessentially American, combining the vibes of New York, San Francisco, and all points in between.

Then came the 20th century. White people got all uppity about sex, drugs, and music. Next thing you know, they outlawed hemp. They tried to outlaw rock 'n' roll. And they nearly wiped out the Moonalice tribe, the remnants of which were forced underground.

Fortunately, a new day has begun. A daring group of nomads has emerged to revive the tribe, its music, and its Legend. The new Moonalice crosses the land, spreading good vibes and giving new hope to millions whose culture had been laid waste by the prohibition of hemp. With each gig, the tribe grows. It turns out there is Moonalice in everyone.

Moonalice legend speaks of a mysterious 7th player — a bass player, naturally — who possesses prodigious talent. The spirit of Yggdrassil Moonalice inhabits all Moonalice gigs. And some times, when the stars, sun, and Moonalice align, Yggdrassil appears in body. And when he does, the tribe rejoices.

It is said by those who say such things that the day will come when all members of the tribe will play bass together. And on that day the notion of low will be taken to new depths. Or possibly the notion of depth taken to new lows. As with all things, it's really a matter of perspective.

* The back story as reported on the Moonalice website.

Moonalice (the band!!!)

Hardwood Moonalice (G.E. Smith) _ bass, guitars, vocals

Jesús H. Moonalice (Barry Sless) _ bass, guitar, pedal steel, vocals

Sir Sinjin Moonalice (Pete Sears) _ bass, keyboards, accordion, vocals

Blue Moonalice (Ann McNamee) _ bass, keyboards, percussion, vocals

Chubby Wombat Moonalice (Roger McNamee) _ bass, guitar, vocals

DawnMan Moonalice (Jimmy Sanchez) _ bass and drums

The Seventh . . . Yggdrassil Moonalice (Jack Casady) _ BASS!!!!!

The Legend on the Road ...

Cannabis Awareness Day (7)
United Nations Plaza, San Francisco, CA

Other Acts: Cold Blood, Nick Gravenites, The Mermen

According to Moonalice legend, early generations of the tribe included both nomads (known as bands) and farmers (known as hippies). The bands and hippies gathered from time to time for pow wows (known as gigs), where the low tones of traditional Moonalice music could be heard for miles around. One of the core Moonalice gig rituals of that era was the peace smoke, initiated by the hippies, which occurred at precisely 4:20 in the afternoon. While the details of the peace smoke have been lost to history, elements of the ritual survive to this day. The first gig of the new tribe of Moonalice occurred in United Nations Plaza in San Francisco on a beautiful Saturday afternoon. Billed as Cannabis Awareness Day, the event was a breathtaking example of truth in advertising. Among the many surprises that afternoon was the appearance of The Seventh. With Yggdrassil in the line-up, the rest of the Moonalice tribe settled into higher-toned instruments and reintroduced Moonalice to the world at large.

1. This Changes Everything
2. Cynical Girl
3. Kick It Open
4. Heart Frozen Up
5. I'm Glad You Think So
6. Crazy In Heaven
7. Who Can Say?
8. Dusty Streets Of Cairo
9. Dance Inside The Lightning
10. Road To Here >
11. Barbary Ellen

introducing

Moonalice 7

COLD BLOOD · NICK GRAVENITES

the MERMEN

CANNABIS DAY 2007

Saturday, May 5th · 1pm

UNITED NATIONS PLAZA

SAN FRANCISCO · CALIFORNIA

"Shoot for the moon. Even if you miss, you'll land among the stars."
-Les Brown

Moonalice

artwork by Chris Shaw

A Celebration of Hope
A Magical Evening To Benefit
Accelerate Brain Cancer Cure

Friday • MAY 11 • 2007   Atherton • California

www.moonaliceband.com

Accelerate Brain Cancer Cure Benefit (7)
Atherton, CA

According to Moonalice legend, music is a life force, animating all things with melody, harmony, and rhythm. It is said that Moonalice music can raise the spirits of the downtrodden and restore the sick to good health. The band carried on the tradition at a benefit for Accelerate Brain Cancer Cure, which raised more than $1.7 million for brain cancer research.

1. This Changes Everything
2. Cynical Girl
3. Kick It Open
4. Heart Frozen Up
5. Can't Help But Wonder Where I'm Bound
6. Get A Little
7. Slow Dance
8. Like A Rolling Stone
9. Crazy In Heaven
10. Who Can Say?
11. Dusty Streets Of Cairo
12. Dance Inside Lightning
13. Goin' Down The Road Feeling Bad

Wavy Gravy's Summer of Love Revival

San Geronimo Valley Community Center, San Geronimo, CA

Other Acts: Summer of Love Revival All-Stars (Barry Melton, Greg Anton, Martin Fierro, Banana, Tom Finch, and more.)

According to Moonalice legend, membership in the tribe has always been a matter of self-selection, rather than birth. While this disqualifies the tribe for casino ownership, it minimizes squabbling at holidays. In the new Moonalice era, the tribe welcomes all fans of low tones. All we ask is that aspiring Moonalice tribe members choose an appropriately humorous moniker.

Wavy Gravy's Summer of Love Revival brought more than 500 new members into the tribe on a chilly day in Marin County. Rotating four players on bass, the band delivered a tasty baker's dozen of songs, including Blink Of An Eye, Moonalice's first studio release.

The afternoon also saw the revival of an ancient Moonalice ritual: mooning the band. True to the ancient custom, the mooner in question did a slow strip tease (revealing a most extraordinary matched set of red and white striped undies), before going for the full Monty. The mooner was also wearing a bright red clown nose . . . it was Wavy!!!

1. This Changes Everything
2. Dusty Streets Of Cairo
3. Kick It Open
4. Slow Dance
5. I'm Glad You Think So
6. Heart Frozen Up
7. Crazy In Heaven
8. Geronimo's Cadillac
9. Blink Of An Eye
10. Dance Inside The Lightning
11. Who Can Say?
12. Barbary Ellen
13. Stella Blue

THE

WAVY GRAVY SUMMER OF LOVE REVIVAL

artwork by Chris Shaw

REVIVAL ALL-STARS

WITH MEMBERS OF: ZERO, BIG BROTHER, JERRY GARCIA BAND,
YOUNGBLOODS, COUNTRY JOE & THE FISH - AND MORE!

MOONALICE &

EUPHORIA

ARTISTS:
WAVY GRAVY • JERRY GARCIA
DAVE SHERIDAN • GILBERT SHELTON
STANLEY MOUSE • MOT • DAVA

www.moonaliceband.com

SAN GERONIMO
VALLEY COMMUNITY CENTER

6350 SIR FRANCIS DRAKE BLVD. SAN GERONIMO - CALIFORNIA • INFO: 415-488-8888 WWW.SGVCC.ORG
$10-$25 SLIDING SCALE • PARTIAL PROCEEDS TO CAMP WINNARAINBOW

SATURDAY
JUNE 2
2007

Jewels in the Square Union Square, San Francisco, CA

According to Moonalice legend, all members of the tribe shall be chiefs, whether or not they play bass. While it is a fact that bass playing is the heart of Moonalice spirituality, it brings with it a heavy amp and a sore back, not a special place in the tribal hierarchy. Evidence of these great truths was on display in Union Square this day, as the band played a lunchtime gig in the heart of San Francisco. A large tribe formed in the Square shortly after noon. In keeping with tribal tradition, everyone was in charge. This produced levels of dancing and carrying on seldom seen in Union Square without intervention from the local constabulary. Other than a touch of sunburn on Chubby Wombat's scalp, no animals (or tribe members) were harmed in the making of this gig.

1. This Changes Everything
2. Dusty Streets Of Cairo
3. Kick It Open
4. Slow Dance
5. I'm Glad You Think So
6. Heart Frozen Up
7. Crazy In Heaven
8. Eileen Aroon
9. Blink Of An Eye
10. Who Can Say?
11. Dance Inside The Lightning
12. Barbary Ellen
13. Goin' Down The Road Feeling Bad

Moonalice ⁶

Jewels
in The Square

Tuesday, June 26 - 2007
Show: 12:30 pm - Free
Union Square - San Francisco - California

www.moonaliceband.com

artwork by Chris Shaw

HOT TUNA

MOONALICE · COLD FLAVOR REPAIR

DR. DAVID E. SMITH & THE DAVID E. SMITH FOUNDATION PRESENT
ROCK & RECOVERY CELEBRATING THE 40TH ANNIVERSARY OF HAIGHT ASHBURY AND SUMMER OF LOVE

WEDNESDAY JUNE 27 2007 · 8PM

WILLIE L. BROWN JR. HIGH AND HIGH SCHOOL AND DR. DAVID E. SMITH, MD

GREAT AMERICAN MUSIC HALL

859 O'FARRELL STREET · SAN FRANCISCO · CALIFORNIA

Rock And Recovery Benefit
Great American Music Hall, San Francisco, CA

Supporting Hot Tuna
Other Acts: Cold Flavor Repair

In Moonalice legend, the medicine man was a bass player who combined great musical skills with a prodigious ability to procure organic materials to take the edge off tribal reality. So powerful was Moonalice medicine that no one could afford it, which gave rise to the Moonalice Free Clinic, which provided drugs and care to those in need. It is said that the whole tribe soon needed care. In modern times, the free clinic movement got second life in San Francisco, where the Haight-Ashbury Free Clinic set a standard of care that is admired and widely imitated. The admiration of the city of San Francisco was reflected in a benefit for Clinic founder David Smith's new program, Rock and Recovery, at the Great American Music Hall, where the band shared the bill with Hot Tuna and Cold Flavor Repair. GAMH offered the perfect setting for a benefit show on a warm Wednesday night. The air was fresh with the smells of summer. Moonalice tribe members attended in large numbers, many sporting stickers saying, "Hi! My name is _____ Moonalice!" The band was pleased to see F. Stop Moonalice, Roadkill Moonalice, P. Bitch Moonalice, Technicolor Moonalice, Captain Moonalice, Chrispy Moonalice, 8-String Moonalice, and many other chiefs. (Thank goodness for name tags!)

1. Cynical Girl
2. Kick It Open
3. I'm Glad You Think So
4. Crazy In Heaven
5. Dusty Streets Of Cairo
6. Who Can Say?
7. Dance Inside The Lightning
8. Heart Frozen Up
9. Blink Of An Eye
10. Goin' Down The Road Feeling Bad

Jewels in the Square Union Square, San Francisco, CA

According to Moonalice legend, the tribe in ancient days wandered the continent in search of spiritual fulfillment. At some point long ago, the tribe found itself in the city of giants, where the gates were golden, the hills steep, and the air filled with aromatic breezes from Humboldt and Mendocino counties. It was there, in the city of St. Francis, that the Moonalice tribe discovered the power of free music. The tribe was told that if it could haul its instruments up the hill known as Nob, there would be a high paying gig at some schmantzy hotel. Years of idleness had taken their toll, however, and the tribe took only one look at the hill before deciding that money was not a good reason to schlep their gear any further. This realization hit the tribe at the corner of Post and Powell Streets, in a public space that was home to the Teamsters and a predecessor to the AFL-CIO. Standing on edge of this Union Square, the tribe found both spiritual fulfillment and the union movement. Soon the low tones of traditional Moonalice music could be heard across the square and there was much joy in city by the bay. The present day tribe of Moonalice gathered on this last day of July of 2007, hoping to recreate the spiritual fulfillment of those days gone by. Under a blazing sun, just after midday, the band did its thing for a squareful of fans. Fulfillment was everywhere. Noting that the Teamsters and AFL-CIO were nowhere to be found in Union Square that day, Chubby Wombat Moonalice offered to acquire some Ex-Lax to get the labor movement started again. The rest, as they say, is legend.

1. This Changes Everything
2. Kick It Open
3. I'm Glad You Think So
4. Dusty Streets Of Cairo
5. Crazy In Heaven
6. Who Can Say?
7. Tell Me It's Okay
8. Barbary Ellen
9. Dance Inside The Lightning
10. Highway 61 Revisited
11. Listen To Those Eyes
12. Goin' Down The Road Feeling Bad

MOONALICE

JEWELS
IN THE SQUARE

TUESDAY, JULY 31 - 2007
SHOW: 12:30 PM - FREE

UNION SQUARE - SAN FRANCISCO - CALIFORNIA

Grateful Garcia Gathering Camp NCN, Black River Falls, WI

Other Acts: Melvin Seals & JGB, Donna Jean & The Tricksters, Boris Garcia

According to Moonalice legend, the ancient tribe consisted of two large groups, the hippies and the bands. Less well known were many smaller groups scattered across the continent. The upper Midwest was home to a group whose existence has been hotly debated by Moonalice scholars everywhere. They were nudists (known as Badgers) and much controversy surrounds them. Drawn by reports of the mild winters and gentle summers of Wisconsin, the Badgers set up clothing optional communities across the state. Imagine their surprise when they saw what Wisconsin winters and summers were really like. It's no surprise that the Badgers proved to be among the hardiest of the Moonalice groups.

The modern Moonalice arrived in Wisconsin for the annual Grateful Garcia Gathering, a two-day festival that included such good friends as Melvin Seals & JGB, Donna Jean and the Tricksters, and Boris Garcia. The festival was at a resort called Camp NCN that is apparently owned by a local tribe of native Americans. We started unpacking gear under a big sign that said, "For Adults Only." Another sign referred to Camp NCN as an "adult camp." It was then that we realized that Camp NCN stood for No Clothing Necessary and that it had once been home to our Moonalice forebears. To the dismay of all, the Grateful Garcia Gathering had rented Camp NCN and suspended local custom in favor of a more traditional tie-dye and jeans motif.

1. Heart Frozen Up
2. Fair To Even Odds
3. Listen To Those Eyes
4. I'm Glad You Think So
5. Dusty Streets Of Cairo
6. Crazy In Heaven
7. Tell Me It's Okay
8. Dance Inside The Lightning
9. Nick Of Time >
10. Blink Of An Eye
11. Let It Rock
12. Barbary Ellen
13. Kick It Open
14. Highway 61 Revisited
15. Stella Blue

Grateful Garcia Gathering

Moonalice

artwork by Chris Shaw

CAMP NCN
8390 Highway 12
Black River Falls • Wisconsin

AUGUST 3rd 2007

AUGUST 4th 2007

www.moonaliceband.com

Grateful Garcia Gathering Camp NCN, Black River Falls, WI

Other Acts: Melvin Seals & JGB, Donna Jean & The Tricksters, Boris Garcia

According to Moonalice legend, tribe members traditionally engaged in two forms of commerce. The bands played music. The hippies grew hemp for ropes and other purposes. Over the centuries, these trades served the tribe very well. However, in modern times the music industry withered and the government stamped out hemp farming. As a result, the modern Moonalice tribe pales by comparison to more prosperous groups of native Americans, such as those in Cleveland, Ohio, whose focus on baseball supports that tribe well. Moonalice's visit to Wisconsin reinforced the band's appreciation of the wiser choices made by other tribes native to the region. Consider, for example, the Ho Chunk Nation, whose casino provided the band with an afternoon of entertainment before this gig. Consider also Wisconsin's own Winnebago tribe, whose high quality RVs continue to be highly prized. At least Moonalice still has its health.

The weather on this day was nasty, but the rain stopped just before the band started and stayed away for the entire set.

1. Cynical Girl
2. Dance Inside The Lightning
3. Tell Me It's Okay
4. Fair To Even Odds
5. This Changes Everything
6. Dusty Streets Of Cairo
7. I'm Glad You Think So
8. Eyesight To The Blind
9. Blink Of An Eye >
10. Nick Of Time
11. Heart Frozen Up
12. Crazy In Heaven
13. Listen To Those Eyes
14. Who Can Say?
15. Sugaree
16. Kick It Open
17. Barbary Ellen
18. Goin' Down The Road Feeling Bad

Alice's Champagne Palace Homer, AK

According to Moonalice legend, tribal members in the far north lived in a picturesque setting with ocean waves beneath towering cliffs topped with expansive glaciers. The natural beauty of Alaska has long been a topic of speculation at tribal conferences, as rainfall and fog have prevented Moonalice visitors from seeing the ocean, mountains, and glaciers — to say nothing of the sky — in recent memory. The modern Moonalice tribe showed up in Homer on a stunning Thursday afternoon. Desperate to verify that it was actually Alaska and not a sound stage at the Walt Disney motion picture studios, we were relieved by the presence of halibut hanging from every nail on the spit, confirming that Moonalice was indeed in Homer. The presence of a huge and boisterous crowd confirmed that we were at Alice's Champagne Palace.

According to Moonalice legend, the last one to sing a song in concert has to play drums. That uncertainty has now been eliminated, as Barry stepped up to the mic for "Dink's Blues."

FIRST SET
1. Heart Frozen Up
2. Crazy In Heaven
3. Fair To Even Odds
4. Tell Me It's Okay
5. This Changes Everything
6. Eyesight To The Blind
7. Slow Dance
8. I'm Glad You Think So
10. Dusty Streets Of Cairo

11. Dance Inside The Lightning
12. Kick It Open
13. Sugaree

SECOND SET
14. Highway 61 Revisited
15. When Will I See You Again? >
16. Cynical Girl
17. Who Can Say?

18. Blink Of An Eye >
19. Nick Of Time
20. Geronimo's Cadillac
21. Barbary Ellen
22. Dink's Blues
23. Listen To Those Eyes
24. Stella Blue
25. Goin' Down The Road Feeling Bad

artwork by Alexandra Fischer

Moonalice

AUGUST 10th 2007

AUGUST 11th 2007

www.moonaliceband.com

Alice's Champagne Palace
195 E. Pioneer Ave • Homer, Alaska

Alice's Champagne Palace Homer, AK

According to Moonalice legend, a great migration took place every spring from tribal freezing grounds in the polar north to the bountiful fields of northern California. No explanation exists for this migration, unless you believe that the tribe was allergic to humpback whales and wanted to stay as far away as possible.

Somewhere along the line, Moonalice hippies discovered hemp, which immediately became the foundation of Moonalice culture. While hemp farming in the Alaska winter never panned out, it prospered in the California summer. Before long, Moonalice villages across California were enhanced with high quality rope, fabrics, and a variety of entertainment products. Before long, tribal members could no longer remember why they had bothered to walk a couple thousand miles just so they could freeze all winter. The rest, as they say, is history.

The search for truth that characterizes the modern Moonalice tribe led the band to make a pilgrimage to Alaska, the Upper One. Armed with bags of winter clothing and enough food to last until dinner, the tribe headed north. Exercising an abundance of caution, we made the trip in mid-summer and found ourselves subjected to the twin hardships of seventy-degree weather and blazing sunshine. Further investigation between sets at Alice's revealed olfactory evidence that hemp farming had made its way to the Kenai Peninsula. How ironic.

FIRST SET

1. This Changes Everything
2. Eyesight To The Blind
3. Fair To Even Odds
4. I'm Glad You Think So
5. Black Is The Color
6. Crazy In Heaven
7. Dusty Streets Of Cairo
8. Listen To Those Eyes
9. Heart Frozen Up
10. Slow Dance
11. Tell Me It's Okay
12. Sugaree
13. Kick It Open

SECOND SET

14. Highway 61 Revisited
15. Blink Of An Eye >
16. Nick Of Time
17. Dink's Blues
18. Dubya
19. When Will I See You Again? >
20. Cynical Girl
21. Let It Rock
22. Barbary Ellen
23. Who Can Say?
24. Dance Inside The Lightning
25. Stella Blue
26. Goin' Down The Road Feeling Bad

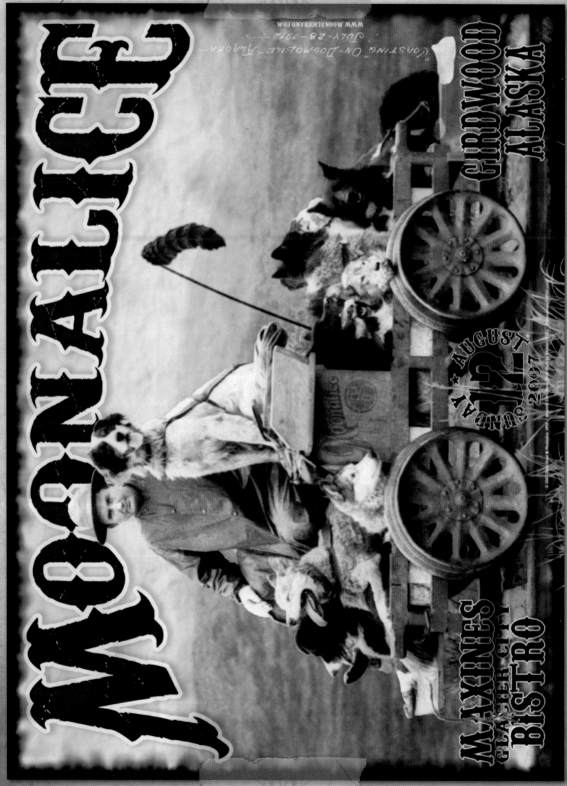

artwork by Chris Shaw

MOONALICE

GIRDWOOD ALASKA

WWW.MOONALICEBAND.COM

"Coasting On Dogmobile Alaska"
"July-28-1912"

AUGUST 12 SUNDAY 2007

MAXINE'S GLACIER CITY BISTRO

Maxine's Glacier City Bistro Girdwood, AK

According to Moonalice legend, all hills are alive with the sound of rock 'n' roll. Alaska's Mount Alyeska is no exception, although skeptics suggest that the tones we are hearing are actually tinnitus. No matter. Maxine's was jammed and our ears are still ringing with jubilant choruses of Goin' Down The Road sung enthusiastically in 200-part harmony. Hardwood called numerous audibles in the set list, introducing an element of danger into an event that already had all the beer it needed. Fortunately no fans or animals were harmed in the making of this gig. Anton and Austen Eriksson sat in and played brilliantly on percussion.

Our drummer, DawnMan Moonalice, who doesn't believe in sleep, went out for an early morning stroll in Girdwood and encountered a mama moose with two pups. For reasons he cannot adequately explain, Dawn Man didn't bring the meeses home with him. He now claims that Moonalice legend does not allow members of the nomadic clan to have pets. Temporarily stunned by the outrage of Moonalice legend being invoked by someone who has never played bass, we recovered more slowly than we would like to admit. You can be sure we're looking into it. No matter what, DawnMan should watch his back. Stay tuned.

FIRST SET
1. This Changes Everything
2. Eyesight To The Blind
3. Fair To Even Odds
4. I'm Glad You Think So
5. Crazy In Heaven
6. Let It Rock
7. Slow Dance
8. Heart Frozen Up
9. Dubya
10. Barbary Ellen
11. Kick It Open
12. Listen To Those Eyes
13. Can't Hold Out
14. Sugaree

SECOND SET
15. Highway 61 Revisited
16. Blink Of An Eye
17. Nick Of Time
18. Dusty Streets Of Cairo
19. Tell Me It's Okay
20. When Will I See You Again? >
21. Cynical Girl
22. Can't Help But Wonder Where I'm Bound
23. Geronimo's Cadillac
24. Who Can Say?
25. Like A Rolling Stone
26. Stella Blue
27. Goin' Down The Road Feeling Bad
28. Mona

KEUL – Alaska Radio *Girdwood, AK*

According to Moonalice legend, the tribe had a long tradition of identifying and caring for unusual species found in nature. In the days before it joined the union in 1959, Alaska was an altered state that was particularly conducive to the discovery of funny critters. For example, Moonalice tribe members discovered that the altered state bird of Alaska was the Common Rhino Puffin, an elusive and barely airworthy seabird with a gnarly horn in the middle of its forehead that it used to spike its prey. The Rhino Puffin's numbers were devastated after 9-11 because of a government crackdown on its violent relative, the Jihadi Rhino Puffin. With several ounces of plastic explosive strapped to its chest, the Jihadi Rhino Puffin terrorized sea life in the Bering Strait, blowing itself up whenever it encountered a school of fish. Despite visible differences between the species, government agents waged puffinocide, making no effort to distinguish between the violent Jihadis and the gentle Common Rhino Puffin. The government-sanctioned massacre depleted the species to the point of extinction.

While no Rhino Puffins have yet been sighted on this Moonalice tour, the band did stop off to visit our old friends at Glacier Radio, KEUL in Girdwood. For the third time in three years the band had great difficulty finding the studio. While KEUL claims that the problem is with Roadkill Moonalice's navigation, the band knows the real story: the former radio pirates at KEUL have at least three identical studios in different parts of Girdwood.

1. Blink Of An Eye
2. Nick Of Time
3. Eileen Aroon
4. Kick It Open
5. Dubya
6. Slow Dance

Hangar On The Wharf Juneau, AK

According to Moonalice legend, leviathans of the sea spent their summers frolicking in Alaska's Inside Passage and their winters in the warm waters off Mexico and Hawaii. We had heard tell that these giant creatures could still be found near Juneau and sent a fact-finding team to confirm the Legend. Expecting to find humongous, ocean going mammals, what they found instead were metal behemoths tied up in the harbor. Apparently these beasts are called "cruise ships." Juneau was crawling with them, without a whale in sight. Could the Legend be mistaken? Impossible. As one would expect, the Moonalice Historical Society has empanelled a committee to look into the so-called facts of the matter. Stay tuned.

1. This Changes Everything
2. Eyesight To The Blind
3. Fair To Even Odds
4. I'm Glad You Think So
5. Black Is The Color
6. Crazy In Heaven
7. Dusty Streets Of Cairo
8. Listen To Those Eyes
9. Heart Frozen Up
10. Slow Dance
11. Dubya
12. Kick It Open
13. Sugaree
14. Highway 61 Revisited
15. Blink Of An Eye
16. Happy Endings
17. When Will I See You Again?
18. Who Can Say?
19. Can't Hold Out
20. Road To Here
21. Dance Inside The Lightning >
22. Jam >
23. Tell Me It's Okay
24. Stella Blue
25. Goin' Down The Road Feeling Bad

MOONALICE

www.moonaliceband.com

AUG. 14   AUG. 15

HANGAR ON THE WHARF
2 MARINE WAY
JUNEAU - ALASKA

artwork by Chris Shaw

Hangar On The Wharf Juneau, AK

According to Moonalice legend, there is no such thing as a turd flower. Not now. Not ever. So what do you call the current inhabitant of the White House? Most people call him Mr. President, but Mr. Turd Flower is a name we heard bandied about in Juneau. This is not the first time we have experienced cognitive dissonance with respect to the Legend. We've taken two extra-strength aspirin _ in gel caps, of course _ but the dissonance remains. We're thinking of going bowling, but don't see how that will resolve the controversy.

This band has only existed for the three months and already the Moonalice legend has developed as many holes as a large slab of Emmenthaler.

1. Barbary Ellen
2. Fair To Even Odds
3. Can't Hold Out
4. Blink Of An Eye
5. Crazy In Heaven
6. I'm Glad You Think So
7. Black Is The Color
8. Dance Inside The Lightning >
9. Tell Me It's Okay
10. Dusty Streets Of Cairo
11. Listen To Those Eyes
12. Let It Rock
13. Who Can Say?
14. Dubya
15. Happy Endings
16. Kick It Open
17. Sugaree
18. Goin' Down The Road Feeling Bad
19. Red House

KHNS – Alaska Radio Haines, AK

According to Moonalice legend, the tribal bands of ancient times played special events in the buff. Legend goes on to say that the audience was naked also. Given the modern Moonalice's recent experience at Camp NCN in Wisconsin, we were less unprepared than we might have been for the sartorial standard – or lack thereof – at KHNS, the radio station in Haines, Alaska. We know it's hard to imagine the employees of a major radio station working in the raw. Harder still to imagine how they persuaded us to play in the raw. Do you have any idea how weird it feels to have an acoustic guitar on your bare skin? Ewwww!

1. Fair To Even Odds
2. Slow Dance
3. Don't Start Me Talking
4. I'm Glad You Think So
5. Eileen Aroon
6. Blink Of An Eye

The Red Onion Skagway, AK

According to Moonalice legend, tribe members answered the siren call of Klondike gold at the end of the 19th century. They headed to the top of the Inside Passage, to the frontier town of Skagway. The tribe members took one look at the trail to gold country and had second thoughts. The trail is about six inches wide and goes straight up for nearly a gazillion miles. Suddenly gold seemed a lot less attractive than the traditional Moonalice trades -- music and hemp. The tribe members quickly discovered that music and hemp were particularly valuable in the port from which miners began the backbreaking journey to gold country.

The modern Moonalice band arrived in Skagway on a beautiful day and immediately headed to the Red Onion. A Skagway fixture from the very beginning, the Onion has a storied history of drunkenness and debauchery. It seemed like the ideal location for a gig. The place is tiny, so the band worked with a Lilliputian backline and no recording equipment. Judging from the general state of inebriation, it's possible that the Onion may have run out of liquor. We lost track of the set list, too, but a reasonable facsimile can be found below . . . Hardwood remembers that we played Mona, but no one can confirm that.

1. Heart Frozen Up
2. Constellation Rag
3. Eyesight To The Blind
4. Fair To Even Odds
5. Like A Rolling Stone
6. I Ain't Ever Satisfied
7. Happy Endings
8. Who Can Say?
9. Messin' With The Kid
10. Dusty Streets Of Cairo
11. Nick Of Time
12. Tell Me It's Okay
13. Too Much Monkey Business
14. Sunnyland
15. Kick It Open
16. I'm Glad You Think So
17. Barbary Ellen
18. Highway 61 Revisited
19. Pete's Boogie
20. Stella Blue
21. Goin' Down The Road Feeling Bad
22. Sugaree

MOONALICE

artwork by Chris Shaw

FRIDAY
AUGUST 17, 2007

the
RED ONION
2nd & BROADWAY
SKAGWAY - ALASKA

WWW.MOONALICEBAND.COM

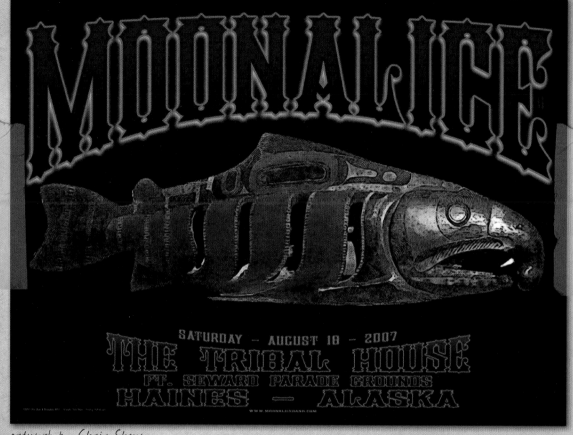

artwork by Chris Shaw

Tribal House Haines, AK

According to Moonalice legend, one branch of the family tree controlled the land around a harbor in what is now the village of Haines. Back in Alaska's early years as an "altered state," they built Castle Moonalice, a fortress so poorly located that it could neither see the harbor from its ramparts nor reach enemy ships with its guns. Castle Moonalice was home to Moon-sshole Moonalice I and his heirs. Moon-sshole I married his sister, beginning a family custom that persisted through twenty-three generations. The last of the line, Moon-sshole XXIII, was such a complete imbecile that he set siege to his own castle, ultimately starving his family and destroying the place. All that remained was the foundation, which was never seen again.

When the modern Moonalice arrived in Haines, the plan was to visit the tomb of Moon-sshole XIII, known to his subjects as Dimwit. The tomb was located in that basement of the Hammer Museum in Haines, under the largest collection of balpeen and claw hammers we've ever seen.

When we played the Tribal House that night, all of Haines was there. The party went on until dawn, at which time everyone stumbled into the parade ground of Haines' historic Fort Seward. There we saw the remains of an army barracks building that burned down a few years ago. Despite the late hour (and other factors), the old foundation rang a bell in our foggy brains. It begged for follow-up research. Two calls to the Moonalice Historical Society confirmed what we had already begun to suspect. The barracks had been built atop the remains of Castle Moonalice! Hard to believe, but there you have it.

1. Dusty Streets Of Cairo
2. Fair To Even Odds
3. I'm Glad You Think So
4. Blink Of An Eye
5. Eyesight To The Blind
6. Happy Endings
7. Crazy In Heaven
8. Messin' With The Kid
9. Dink's Blues
10. Who Can Say?
11. Black Is The Color
12. Nick Of Time
13. Slow Dance
14. Heart Frozen Up
15. Dance Inside The Lightning
16. Tell Me It's Okay
17. Kick It Open
18. Barbary Ellen
19. Listen To Those Eyes
20. Can't Hold Out
21. Stella Blue
22. Goin' Down The Road Feeling Bad
23. Sugaree

Jewels in the Square Union Square, San Francisco, CA

According to Moonalice legend, the Coming of the Seventh will be preceded by the Introduction of the Fifth. Every Moonalice schoolchild knows the Seventh to be Yggdrassil, a bass player of such prodigious talent that he causes all other bass players to take up different instruments. But who or what is the Fifth? Such a mystery!!! Could it be a bottle of scotch consumed by disappointed band members who have been forced to give up their four-stringed instruments in favor of those with six or eighty-eight strings? Or could it be something else? The mystery has finally been solved. At rehearsal for this gig in Union Square, Blue Moonalice, the distaff member of the band, took up the bass for the very first time. She was the fifth member of the modern Moonalice troupe to perform on the exalted instrument. Showing a technique that may one day revolutionize bass playing, Blue riffed like a madwoman, causing some to wonder what the big deal is with this Yggdrassil guy. Moonalice insiders know the truth. Yggdrassil is Jack Casady, who will rejoin Moonalice later this week in Santa Cruz. As a result, the gig in Union Square was the last chance that Chubby Wombat and Hardwood had to play the low tones for awhile. CW and Hardwood may be done, but they didn't go quietly. Every knob was turned up to 11.

1. Heart Frozen Up
2. Fair To Even Odds
3. Crazy In Heaven
4. Happy Endings
5. Eyesight To The Blind
6. Blink Of An Eye
7. Kick It Open
8. Listen To Those Eyes
9. Dusty Streets Of Cairo
10. Dance Inside The Lightning >
11. Tell Me It's Okay
12. Sugaree

MOONALICE

7

TUESDAY, AUGUST 28, 2007 · 12:30 PM · FREE!
JEWELS IN THE SQUARE
UNION SQUARE · SAN FRANCISCO

©2007 Chris Shaw & Moonalice 2007 · Art: Chris Shaw · Printed @ www.xagent.com

WWW.MOONALIVEBAND.COM

45

artwork by Alexandra Fischer

MOONALICE

C.E. Smith, Jack Casady, Barry Sless, Pete Sears, Ann McNamee, Roger McNamee, Jimmy Sanchez

WWW.MOONALICEBAND.COM

AUGUST 31ST 2007

MOE'S ALLEY
1535 COMMERCIAL WAY • SANTA CRUZ, CALIFORNIA

KPIG Freedom, CA

According to Moonalice legend, all pigs are created equal. In modern times, however, one pig is more equal than others. That pig is KPIG, where the band stopped in for a short set on the way to Moe's Alley. In a cozy studio masquerading as a motel, KPIG provides an oasis of great music in the increasingly yack-filled world of FM radio. Apparently that is part of Moonalice legend, too.

1. Kick It Open
2. Slow Dance
3. Dusty Streets Of Cairo

Moe's Alley (7) Santa Cruz, CA   8-31-07

According to Moonalice legend, the Coming of the Seventh will be a cause for much rejoicing in the tribe. While the ceremonial details have been lost to the fog of history, Legend has it that the arrival of the Seventh generally involves much drinking, dancing, and carrying on. In short, the Coming of the Seventh is like any other Moonalice celebration, only more so. And so it was this Friday night in Santa Cruz. Yggdrassil Moonalice returned to the band, bringing with him an extraordinary range of low tones, to say nothing of wisdom and cool eyebrows. To the surprise of no one, there was much drinking, dancing, and carrying on.

FIRST SET
1. Eyesight To The Blind
2. Crazy In Heaven
3. I'm Glad You Think So
4. Love in Vain
5. Fair To Even Odds
6. Barbary Ellen
7. Blink Of An Eye
8. Cynical Girl
9. Road To Here >
10. Jumpin' Jack Flash
11. Who Can Say?
12. Messin' With The Kid
13. Happy Endings

SECOND SET
14. Highway 61 Revisited
15. Goin' Down The Road Feeling Bad
16. Heart Frozen Up
17. Like A Rolling Stone
18. Stella Blue
19. Tell Me It's Okay
20. Sugaree

Sausalito Arts Festival (7) Marinship Park, Sausalito, CA

Other Acts: Jefferson Starship, Quicksilver Messenger Service, It's A Beautiful Day

According to Moonalice legend, the ancient tribal occupations of hemp farming and music produced great harmony. Such was the energy of the tribe in ancient times that it created hemp and music in prodigious volumes. Happiness reigned supreme in the tribe, which partied continuously for the better part of a millennium, until everyone finally ran out rope and other hemp derivatives. Hemp grew naturally throughout the land, but it didn't harvest itself. For that, hard labor was required. Not much labor, but hard. Just a few days a year. No one was happy about having to break up the party for something as unseemly as work, but the tribal elders could see no way around it. So they created Labor Day Weekend. For three long days in early September, the tribe went into the fields and picked. It was a pain, but the output lasted until the following year. Next thing you know, everybody was celebrating Labor Day. You can look it up.

1. Dusty Streets Of Cairo
2. Dance Inside The Lightning
3. Kick It Open
4. Love In Vain
5. Crazy In Heaven
6. Stella Blue
7. Tell Me It's Okay
8. Sugaree

MOONalice

Jefferson Starship

Quicksilver Messenger Service

David LaFlamme & Friends

Tom Constanten

MAIN STAGE
Saturday
1st
SEPTEMBER
2007

SAUSALITO ARTS FESTIVAL
MARINSHIP PARK · SAUSALITO · CALIFORNIA

artwork by Chris Shaw

www.mooraliceband.com

©2007 Chris Shaw & Moonalice 2007 · Artwork: Chris Shaw · Printing: www.PsPrint.com

Sawtooth Ridge Café (7) Tahoe City, CA

According to Moonalice legend, the tribal hierarchy in ancient times was determined by height and altitude. Not surprisingly, this conveyed great power (known in tribal circles as "buzz") to those who inhabited mountain regions. The band's gig in Tahoe City indicated that nothing has changed. The Labor Day Weekend crowd at the Sawtooth Ridge had a buzz on that could only have been earned through determination and hard work. We were happy to provide the soundtrack for an evening of joyous revelry.

FIRST SET
1. Eyesight To The Blind
2. Crazy In Heaven
3. I'm Glad You Think So
4. Love In Vain
5. Fair To Even Odds
6. Barbary Ellen
7. Blink Of An Eye
8. Cynical Girl
9. Road To Here >
10. Jumpin' Jack Flash
11. When Will I See You Again?
12. Cynical Girl
13. Who Can Say?
14. Black Is The Color
15. Happy Endings
16. Messin' With The Kid
17. Goin' Down The Road Feeling Bad

SECOND SET
18. Too Much Monkey Business
19. Listen To Those Eyes
20. Nick Of Time
21. Kick It Open
22. Slow Dance
23. Let It Rock
24. Stella Blue
25. Sugaree
26. Encore: Tell Me It's Okay

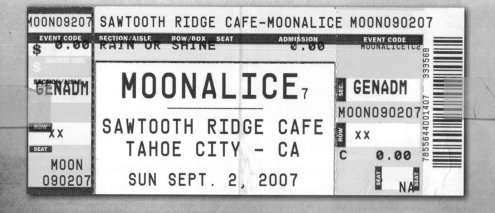

SAWTOOTH RIDGE CAFE-MOONALICE MOON090207

MOON09207 | EVENT CODE | SECTION/AISLE | ROW/BOX | SEAT | ADMISSION | EVENT CODE
$ 0.00 | RAIN OR SHINE | 0.00 | MOONALICETC2

MOONALICE 7
SAWTOOTH RIDGE CAFE
TAHOE CITY - CA
SUN SEPT. 2, 2007

SEC. GENADM
MOON090207
ROW xx
C 0.00
SEAT NA

333568
7855644001407

MOONALICE

artwork by Chris Shaw

SUNDAY
2ND
SEPTEMBER

SAWTOOTH RIDGE CAFE
TAHOE CITY · CALIFORNIA

CNBC "Power Lunch" (7) Hyde Street Pier, San Francisco, CA

According to Moonalice legend, television is the hemp of the missus, as she is the one tied to the remote. On this lovely morning in San Francisco, the tribe transformed itself into the Friday Morning Live Band for a road trip edition of CNBC's top rated show, Power Lunch. Chubby Wombat Moonalice's fur was flying as he was interviewed from the poop deck of a tall ship that resides at Hyde Street Pier. The band played five "bumps" – 15-second fragments of songs – designed to lessen the trauma of the advertising to follow. We also played a full version of Nick Of Time and a four-song dessert that followed Power Lunch

BROADCAST SET
1. Dusty Streets Of Cairo (partial)
2. Kick It Open (partial)
3. Slow Dance (partial)
4. Blues In G (partial)
5. Nick Of Time
6. Blink Of An Eye (partial)

AFTER-SHOW SET
7. Blink Of An Eye
8. Dusty Streets Of Cairo
9. Fair To Even Odds
10. Tell Me It's Okay

MOONALICE
CNBC LIVE
HYDE STREET PIER
SEPTEMBER 14, 2007

0000420

0000420

• CNBC POWER LUNCH •

MOONALICE

HERCULES

FRIDAY • SEPTEMBER 14 • 2007 • 9AM
HYDE STREET PIER
SAN FRANCISCO • CALIFORNIA

artwork by Chris Shaw

MOONALICE

**SATURDAY
SEPTEMBER
15
2007**
WWW.MOONALICEBAND.COM

BIG SKY RESORT
BIG SKY - MONTANA

Big Sky Resort (7) Big Sky, MT

According to Moonalice legend, the higher the audience, the better the band sounds. In ancient times, Moonalice bands and Moonalice hippies lived in harmony, sharing low tones and hemp derivatives to mutual benefit. In modern times, no audience has been higher for a Moonalice show than the one in Big Sky. The stage was 7,200 feet above sea level!!! And the stage was actually the lowest point in the amphitheater. Moonalice legend says little about thin air, but the band did some training at the gig in Tahoe City, where the elevation was 6,000 feet. Chubby Wombat is convinced that audiences are hogging all the oxygen at these high elevation venues. No matter. The Legend proved correct again, as Big Sky's audience helped the band play at an elevated level. Showtime was 6pm, a twilight hour in the mountains, pretty much as late as a band can play outdoors in Big Sky without freezing to death. The mountain rocked . . . it's part of the Legend.

1. Eyesight To The Blind
2. Crazy In Heaven
3. I'm Glad You Think So
4. Black Is The Color
5. Fair To Even Odds
6. Barbary Ellen
7. Blink Of An Eye
8. Cynical Girl
9. Road To Here >
10. Jumpin' Jack Flash
11. Goin' Down The Road Feeling Bad
12. Messin' With The Kid
13. Dance Inside The Lightning
14. Happy Endings
15. Highway 61 Revisited
16. Like A Rolling Stone
17. Heart Frozen Up
18. Kick It Open
19. Stella Blue
20. Tell Me It's Okay
21. Sugaree

artwork by Chris Shaw

MOONALICE 2007

JEWELS IN THE SQUARE

TUESDAY 25 SEPTEMBER 2007
12:30PM - FREE!
www.moonaliceband.com

UNION SQUARE - SAN FRANCISCO - CALIFORNIA

Jewels in the Square (7) Union Square, San Francisco, CA

According to Moonalice legend, there is a happy party ground where tribe members find spiritual fulfillment. No one knows what happens at the happy party ground, but it must be good, as no tribe member is known to have left it. Some students of the Moonalice legend have suggested that the primary activities are pinochle and basket weaving. Others have talked of experimentation with wild mushrooms and smoked items. Fish, for example. Our final Jewels show of the season occurred at lunch time on a beautiful Tuesday. The square was filled, except for an area on the west side where the city has put a huge Zen garden. Faced with a choice between raking rocks and playing music, the band opted for music, as did the audience.

1. Nick Of Time
2. Eyesight To The Blind
3. Fair To Even Odds
4. Blink Of An Eye
5. Road To Here >
6. Jumpin' Jack Flash
7. Dance Inside The Lightning
8. Dusty Streets Of Cairo
9. Crazy In Heaven
10. I'm Glad You Think So
11. Listen To Those Eyes
12. Heart Frozen Up
13. Stella Blue
14. Sugaree
15. Tell Me It's Okay

artwork by Chris Shaw

MOONALICE

THE CANYON CLUB
AT THE FOUR QUEENS HOTEL & CASINO · 202 FREMONT STREET
LAS VEGAS · NEVADA

www.moonaliceband.com

The Canyon Club (7) Las Vegas, NV

Other Acts: The Melancholics

According to Moonalice legend, gambling is not an approved tribal activity. There was a time – ages ago – when the ancient Moonalice tribe gave casino gambling a try, but it didn't work out. Members of the tribe opened a Three-Card Monty parlor in Nevada, but lost so much money the first night that they closed the place down and left the state. In modern times, the Moonalice band received a gracious invitation from the Las Vegas Jam Band Society to play a gig at the Four Queens Hotel. Only after our manager checked to make sure there was no way to bet on Three-Card Monty did we accept. Boy, are we glad we did. The Canyon Club is a terrific venue, with sofas, overstuffed chairs, a really nice sound system, and lots of music fans. Under the watchful eye of Roadkill Moonalice, the tribe managed to leave Sin City with wallets intact.

1. Nick Of Time
2. Eyesight To The Blind
3. Fair To Even Odds
4. Crazy In Heaven
5. Dusty Streets Of Cairo
6. I'm Glad You Think So
7. Happy Endings
8. Kick It Open
9. Somebody To Love
10. Slow Dance
11. Let It Rock
12. Distance
13. Messin' With The Kid
14. Dance Inside The Lightning
15. Stella Blue
16. Tell Me It's Okay
17. Sugaree
18. Goin' Down The Road Feeling Bad

Hardly Strictly Bluegrass Festival (7)
Golden Gate Park, San Francisco, CA

According to Moonalice legend, there is a correlation between the size of any tribal gathering and the quality of the music. In Moonalice-speak, the bigger the pow wow, the deeper the groove. Someone may even have said, "da bigga da bottom, da betta da buzz" but until October 7, we had no confirmation. Hardly Strictly Bluegrass is a small slice of heaven that appears in San Francisco every October. This year there were 72 bands on six stages over two and a half days. And it's all free, thanks to the generosity of Warren Hellman, banjo-picker extraordinaire. The Moonalice band played a 45-minute set at noon on a beautiful Sunday to an audience that numbered somewhere between 10,000 and 30,000. As pow wows go, this one was huge, as was the groove. If you don't believe us, check out the recording.

1. Distance
2. I'm Glad You Think So
3. Dusty Streets Of Cairo
4. Slow Dance
5. Somebody To Love
6. Stella Blue
7. Sugaree

MOONALICE 7

Hardly Strictly Bluegrass Festival

Golden Gate Park
San Francisco

7 October 2007

G.E. Smith
Jack Casady
Barry Sless
Pete Sears
Ann McNamee
Roger McNamee
Jimmy Sanchez

artwork by David Singer

www.moonaliceband.com

Oriental Theater
12 October 2007

Cervantes
Masterpiece Ballroom
13 October 2007

MOONALICE₇

Denver
Colorado

artwork by David Singer

Oriental Theater (7) Denver, CO

Other Acts: Great American Taxi

According to Moonalice legend, the tribe would throw a great party any time a large mountain range crushes a rattlesnake. We had absolutely no idea what this meant until we arrived in Denver on October 12. That night, the local baseball team, the Rockies, beat the Arizona Diamondbacks in the first game of what would ultimately be a four game sweep. While hardly a eureka moment to rival Archimedes in the bathtub, it was a big one by our standards. So was the gig at the Oriental.

1. Distance
2. Eyesight To The Blind
3. Fair To Even Odds
4. Crazy In Heaven
5. Nick Of Time
6. Blink Of An Eye
7. Dusty Streets Of Cairo
8. I'm Glad You Think So
9. Happy Endings
10. Kick It Open
11. Somebody To Love
12. Slow Dance
13. Let It Rock
14. Messin' With The Kid
15. Dance Inside The Lightning
16. Stella Blue
17. Tell Me It's Okay
18. Sugaree
19. Goin' Down The Road Feeling Bad

Cervantes Masterpiece Ballroom (7) Denver, CO 10-13-07

Other Acts: Storytyme

According to Moonalice legend, the pioneers in Denver, Colorado arrived to find the place inhabited by a small group of native American farmers cultivating an indigenous plant with many uses. The farmers were members of the Moonalice tribe. The crop in question is well known to all students of the Moonalice legend. The white men (and women) found many uses for the crop and for many it remains a staple of life in the Rockies. At least that's what we're told . . .

1. Distance
2. Black Is The Color
3. Listen To Those Eyes
4. Fair To Even Odds
5. Barbary Ellen
6. Road To Here >
7. Jumpin' Jack Flash
8. Crazy In Heaven
9. Kick It Open
10. Heart Frozen Up
11. Dance Inside The Lightning
12. Tell Me It's Okay
13. Bleeding Of Love
14. Highway 61 Revisited
15. Stella Blue
16. Like A Rolling Stone
17. Sugaree

The Goodfoot (7) Portland, OR

Other Acts: Furious Jones

According to Moonalice legend, rainfall makes you smarter. Lots of rain makes you much smarter. The rain in Portland is off the scale, which suggests that the people there are brilliant. The band's experience bears this out. Seriously. That's how it is. You guys in the desert are at a big disadvantage. That's what the Legend says. You can look it up.

1. Distance
2. Can't Hold Out
3. Crazy In Heaven
4. Fair To Even Odds
5. I'm Glad You Think So
6. Heart Frozen Up
7. Blink Of An Eye
8. Kick It Open
9. Happy Endings
10. Black Is The Color
11. Bleeding Of Love
12. Dusty Streets Of Cairo
13. Dance Inside The Lightning
14. Tell Me It's Okay
15. Barbary Ellen
16. Stella Blue
17. Somebody To Love
18. Goin' Down The Road Feeling Bad

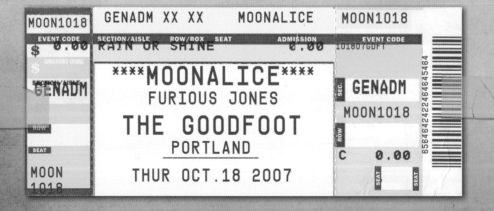

MOONALICE

with Furious Jones

artwork by Chris Shaw

THE GOODFOOT
2845 S.E. STARK · PORTLAND · OREGON

THURSDAY
OCTOBER 18th, 2007

www.moonaliceband.com

artwork by Chris Shaw

Moonalice

The Nectar Lounge

412 North 38th St. - Seattle, Washington

Marcus Eaton

Friday, October 19th, 2007

Nectar Lounge (7) Seattle, WA

Other Acts: Marcus Eaton

According to Moonalice legend, tribe members believed in a metaphysical oasis where music would be combined with pizza to induce a euphoria that would last all night. The oasis was known to the tribe as a "lounge." The band's Northwest tour included two lounge gigs – in Portland and Seattle – and a veritable cornucopia of euphoria. Seattle was especially euphoric, thanks to a large and rowdy audience and the leftover euphoria from the prior night's show in Portland.

1. Distance
2. Highway 61 Revisited
3. Listen To Those Eyes
4. Kick It Open
5. Slow Dance
6. Geronimo's Cadillac
7. I'm Glad You Think So
8. Fair To Even Odds
9. Dance Inside The Lightning
10. Messin' With The Kid
11. Nick Of Time
12. Who Can Say?
13. Crazy In Heaven
14. Dusty Streets Of Cairo
15. Bleeding Of Love
16. Tell Me It's Okay
17. Road To Here >
18. Jumpin' Jack Flash
19. Stella Blue
20. Sugaree
21. Somebody To Love

The Mobius (7) Ashland, OR

According to Moonalice legend, there's no bidness like show bidness. That's right! It's like no bidness we know. The lovely city of Ashland proved the point by simulcasting our shows on the web to a global audience. (We had a viewer in the Ivory Coast!!!!) Now that's show bidness!

1. Distance
2. Eyesight To The Blind
3. Fair To Even Odds
4. Blink Of An Eye
5. I'm Glad You Think So
6. Heart Frozen Up
7. Crazy In Heaven
8. Kick It Open
9. Happy Endings
10. Black Is The Color
11. Bleeding Of Love
12. Dusty Streets Of Cairo
13. Tell Me It's Okay
14. Barbary Ellen
15. Stella Blue
16. Dance Inside The Lightning
17. Somebody To Love
18. Goin' Down The Road Feeling Bad

10-21-07

According to Moonalice legend, the white men who settled in what is now Ashland, OR were greeted by the local chief, Shakespeare Moonalice. Ol' Shakespeare fancied himself as a thespian and taught the white men to appreciate the finer points of dramatic exposition. His influence on Ashland was profound and his legacy can be seen today in the local Best Western that bears his likeness. There's also a festival.

1. Nick Of Time
2. Kick It Open
3. Crazy In Heaven
4. Empire State
5. Constellation Rag
6. Fair To Even Odds
7. Slow Dance
8. Heart Frozen Up
9. Dubya
10. Unspoken Words
11. Bleeding Of Love
12. Junko Partner
13. Dance Inside The Lightning
14. Tell Me It's Okay
15. Codeine
16. Listen To Those Eyes
17. Happy Endings
18. Stella Blue
19. Highway 61 Revisited
20. Somebody To Love
21. Dink's Blues

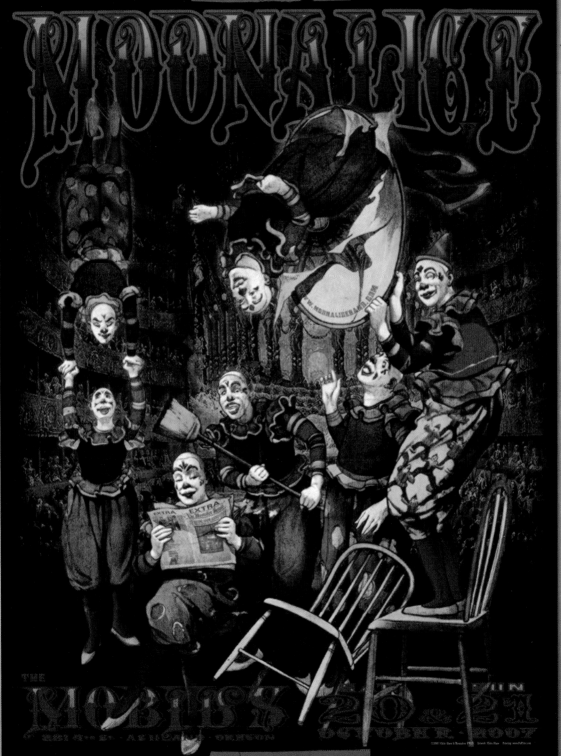

artwork by David Singer

TRUSTe 10th Anniversary Gala
with
MOONALICE

G. E. Smith
Jack Casady
Barry Sless
Pete Sears
Ann McNamee
Roger McNamee
Jimmy Sanchez

22 October 2007

DeYoung Museum

Golden Gate Park • San Francisco • California

www.moonaliceband.com

Special Event (7) - TRUSTe 10th Anniversary Gala
DeYoung Museum in Golden Gate Park, San Francisco, CA

According to Moonalice legend, privacy ceremonies have been central to the tribal experience from its earliest days. The ceremonies began as a form of hide and seek, with everyone running in different directions and not coming back until dinner. Over the years, Moonalice privacy ceremonies evolved with technology. Fire and the wheel led to particularly compelling innovations. It's hard to overstate the importance of fire in Moonalice culture, particularly with respect to the consumption of certain agricultural products ... but subsequent technologies had an impact, as well.

In recent times, the forces of darkness have attacked the tribe, invading its privacy from every direction. Fortunately, TRUSTe emerged in 1997 to defend the tribe (and everyone else) from web-based attacks. While TRUSTe has not yet eliminated all threats to the tribe's privacy, it's the best hope we have.

1. Distance
2. Crazy In Heaven
3. Fair To Even Odds
4. Black Is The Color
5. Constellation Rag
6. Bleeding Of Love
7. Dusty Streets Of Cairo
8. Nick Of Time
9. Kick It Open
10. Somebody To Love
11. Sugaree

artwork by Chris Shaw

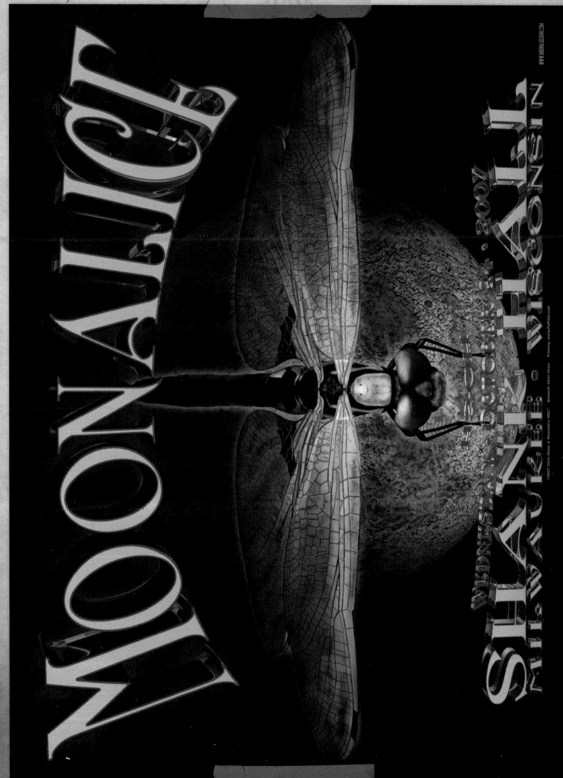

MOONALICE

SHANK HALL · MILWAUKEE · WISCONSIN

Shank Hall (7) Milwaukee, WI

According to Moonalice legend, beer goes really well with hemp. Tribe members in the upper Midwest discovered this in the 19th century, when a bunch of European immigrants with funny names moved into the neighborhood and started brewing. Blatz, Schlitz, and Miller settled in Milwaukee. Their insistence on the use of hops instead of hemp surprised the local Moonalice tribe, but their disappointment didn't last long, as the symbiosis between beer and hemp quickly became obvious to all. Pretty soon thereafter, the tribe discovered German sausages. Hmm-mm good.

Shank Hall is the successor to one of the core locations in the tribe's favorite film, This Is Spinal Tap. Stonehenge – the 18-inch version from the movie – is now suspended over the drum riser, which did wonders for the Big Bottom at our show.

1. Distance
2. Fair To Even Odds
3. Eyesight To The Blind
4. Dance Inside The Lightning
5. Nick Of Time
6. Blink Of An Eye
7. Dusty Streets Of Cairo
8. I'm Glad You Think So
9. Happy Endings
10. Kick It Open
11. Crazy In Heaven
12. Somebody To Love
13. Slow Dance
14. Mona
15. Unspoken Words
16. Messin' With The Kid
17. Bleeding Of Love
18. Stella Blue
19. Tell Me It's Okay
20. Jumpin' Jack Flash
21. Goin' Down The Road Feeling Bad

artwork by Chris Shaw

MOONALICE

THE BRIARS

OCTOBER 25 2007

CHICAGO ILLINOIS

Martyrs (7) Chicago, IL

According to Moonalice legend, the tribe figured prominently in the history of the Windy City. We did some research and discovered that Moonalice's impact on Chicago was sometimes a mixed blessing. For example, the ne'er-do-well Cletus "Sparky" Moonalice was a 19th Century Cow Whisperer who was working for a woman named O'Leary when things went terribly wrong. Whispers turned to yelling. Sparks turned to flames. Chicago burned to the ground. Burdened by this knowledge, the band showed up at Martyrs, determined to make it up to the city of Chicago.

1. Distance
2. Can't Hold Out
3. Crazy In Heaven
4. Fair To Even Odds
5. Constellation Rag
6. Blink Of An Eye
7. Heart Frozen Up
8. Road To Here >
9. Jumpin' Jack Flash
10. Kick It Open
11. Dance Inside The Lightning
12. I Ain't Ever Satisfied
13. Like A Rolling Stone
14. Listen To Those Eyes
15. Too Much Monkey Business
16. Tell Me It's Okay
17. Bleeding Of Love
18. Somebody To Love
19. Happy Endings
20. Barbary Ellen
21. Stella Blue
22. Highway 61 Revisited

The Thirsty Ear (7) Columbus, OH

According to Moonalice legend, the tribe has long encouraged the provision of aid and comfort to creatures with very large heads. We would love this idea no matter what, but really big heads are a Moonalice genetic trait, so we have to like them as a matter of tribal loyalty.

We are reminded of big heads each year during football season, when every college team plays under the control of some critter that looks like what Van Gogh would have painted if he had visited Easter Island. When the band arrived in Columbus, home of the #1 Buckeyes, we were greeted by the Mascot-in-Chief of the local football squad. Brutus Buckeye has a very large head. Apparently it got that way because Brutus holds his breath after inhailing. We can help with that, but what is this Buckeye thing? Is it a shiner? A nut? A flavor of hemp? Curious legends want to know.

1. Distance
2. Eyesight To The Blind
3. Fair To Even Odds
4. Crazy In Heaven
5. I'm Glad You Think So
6. Dusty Streets Of Cairo
7. Blink Of An Eye
8. Nick Of Time
9. Kick It Open
10. Junko Partner
11. Dance Inside The Lightning
12. Happy Endings
13. Heart Frozen Up
14. Stella Blue
15. Tell Me It's Okay
16. Listen To Those Eyes
17. Geronimo's Cadillac
18. Like A Rolling Stone
19. Bleeding Of Love
20. Goin' Down The Road Feeling Bad

Gory at the Quarry (7) Nelson Ledges Quarry Park, Garrettsville, OH

Other Acts: Ekoostik Hookah, Particle, RAQ, Great American Taxi

According to Moonalice legend, Halloween falls at the end of October because it's too cold in November to go door-to-door for candy. In some parts of North America even October is too late. The tribe in Ohio lobbied for years to move Halloween into July to optimize both the weather and the hours of daylight, but they were overruled by the forces of tradition. Too bad. Nelson Ledges Quarry Park is beautiful. On this day, it was cold and rainy, which was hard on our fingers, but had zero impact on the audience, whose enthusiasm and costumes reflected their Moonalice heritage.

1. Somebody To Love
2. Dance Inside The Lightning
3. Fair To Even Odds
4. Happy Endings
5. Dusty Streets Of Cairo
6. Listen To Those Eyes
7. Tell Me It's Okay
8. Stella Blue
9. Bleeding Of Love
10. Sugaree

GORY AT THE QUARRY #11

MOONALICE

G.E. SMITH · JACK CASADY · BARRY SLESS · PETE SEARS · ANN McNAMEE · ROGER McNAMEE · JIMMY SANCHEZ

EKOOSTIK HOOKAH

PARTICLE

GREAT AMERICAN TAXI

RAQ

SATURDAY · OCTOBER 27 · 2007

NELSON LEDGES QUARRY PARK
GARRETTESVILLE · OHIO

www.moonaliceband.com

artwork by Chris Shaw

nov 2007

moonalice

g.e. smith · jack casady · barry sless · pete sears · ann mcnamee · roger mcnamee · jimmy sanchez

the rockhopper all-stars

harpers ferry

158 brighton ave · allston · mass

Harpers Ferry (7) Alston, MA, Other Acts: Rockhopper All-Stars

According to Moonalice legend, the Boston Tea Party story is phony. Like you, we were surprised to discover this, but the Legend is quite specific. History books claim that a group of patriots dressed up as Indians rowed across Boston harbor to a British ship loaded with tea. They climbed aboard, found the cargo of tea and dumped it in the harbor to protest British taxation.

Moonalice legend offers a very different version. Apparently, a group of young tribe members heard that a ship had arrived in Boston to deliver a large cargo of hemp products. When the captain refused to offload the cargo, the tribe boarded the ship to take possession of their hemp. Only after much smoking and coughing did they learn that the cargo was actually tea. In a fit of pique, they dumped it overboard. Patriot leaders saw the tea crates floating in the harbor and quickly claimed credit, citing the tax rebellion. The rest, as they say, is legend.

1. Distance
2. Eyesight To The Blind
3. Fair To Even Odds
4. Listen To Those Eyes
5. I'm Glad You Think So
6. I Ain't Ever Satisfied
7. Kick It Open
8. Blink Of An Eye
9. Nick Of Time
10. Junko Partner
11. Crazy In Heaven
12. Happy Endings
13. Heart Frozen Up
14. Wake Up Little Susie*
15. Train Don't Come Here No Mo'
16. Somebody To Love
17. Constellation Rag
18. Bleeding Of Love
19. Stella Blue
20. Highway 61 Revisited >
21. Done Somebody Wrong
22. Goin' Down The Road Feeling Bad**

*with Lorin and Chris Rowan (Rowan Bros.) on guitar and vocals
**with Giles McNamee on vocals

MOONALICE

INTER-MEDIA ARTS CENTER
HUNTINGTON · LONG ISLAND · NEW YORK

2 NOVEMBER 2007

artwork by David Singer

82

Inter-Media Arts Center (7) Huntington, NY

Other Acts: Taylor Barton

According to Moonalice legend, the great patriot George Washington was a member of the tribe. Everyone knows he was a Mason and our first president, but his role in the Moonalice legend has been obscured by the passage of time. It turns out that after chopping down the cherry tree and not lying about it, George was sent off to spend some time with the Moonalice tribe in Northern Virginia. They taught him how to be a farmer — a hippie, if you will — and George went on to a distinguished career as a plantation owner.

Contrary to popular wisdom, much of the Washington plantation was devoted the cultivation of America's most important indigenous crop, hemp. Given the critical nature of hemp in the economy of the period, it was natural that a hippie such as Washington would be put in charge of first the army and then the country as a whole. While people were less uptight in those days than they are today, they nonetheless used a code to let the general know when they were in need of additional hemp products. The code, which is still in use today, was brilliant in its simplicity. If you needed supplies, you put up a sign that said, "George Washington slept here." Judging by the signs around Huntington, demand for hemp products appears to be very strong.

1. Distance
2. Crazy In Heaven
3. Fair To Even Odds
4. Constellation Rag
5. Can't Hold Out
6. Listen To Those Eyes
7. Like A Rolling Stone
8. Messin' With The Kid
9. Kick It Open
10. Slow Dance
11. Nick Of Time
12. Dusty Streets Of Cairo
13. Dance Inside The Lightning
14. Dink's Blues
15. Somebody To Love
16. Happy Endings
17. Stella Blue
18. Bleeding Of Love
19. Sugaree
20. Goin' Down The Road Feeling Bad*

*with Rob Barracco (Dark Star Orchestra) on vocals and keyboards and Erin Hill on harmony vocals.

Mexicali Blues (7) Teaneck, NJ

According to Moonalice legend, the river's edge in northern New Jersey was home to a major tribal trading center. The village of Hempneck was legendary for its harvest pow wow, Big Bud, a 40-day smokefest that drew thousands. Our research revealed that fossilized roaches were found during the pre-construction excavation at what is now Mexicali Blues, indicating that this may have been the site of ancient Big Bud pow wows. Further research revealed that prissy Brits stamped out the Big Bud in the early 18th century. Whether this was to control the natives or to take the product for themselves remains unclear. What is clear is that the British changed the name of the town to Teaneck, and American patriots rebelled. Led by noted hemp farmer George Washington, the colonists staged a revolution to protect life, liberty, and the pursuit of happiness. In retrospect, the whole revolution thing makes way more sense in the context of this vital fact. Think about it. Why would anyone start a war over tea? It had to be over something way cooler than tea. Duh.

1. Distance
2. Crazy In Heaven
3. Fair To Even Odds
4. Eyesight To The Blind
5. I'm Glad You Think So
6. Ain't Ever Satisfied
7. Blink Of An Eye
8. Nick Of Time
9. Listen To Those Eyes
10. Road To Here >
11. Jumpin' Jack Flash
12. Kick It Open
13. Happy Endings
14. Barbary Ellen
15. Dance Inside The Lightning
16. Somebody To Love*
17. Constellation Rag*
18. Messin' With The Kid*
19. Tell Me It's Okay*
20. Stella Blue*
21. Bleeding Of Love*
22. Sugaree*
23. Like A Rolling Stone*

*with Barry Mitterhoff (Hot Tuna) on mandolin

MOONALICE

SAT 3 NOV
www.moonaliceband.com

MEXICALI BLUES · TEANECK · NEW JERSEY

artwork by Chris Shaw and Alexandra Fischer

7

MOONALICE

EILEN JEWELL

SUNDAY · NOVEMBER 4 · 2007
RAMS HEAD
ANNAPOLIS · MARYLAND

2007 CHRIS SHAW & MOONALICE 2014   ARTWORK: CHRIS SHAW   PRINTING: WWW.PSPRINT.COM

Rams Head (7) Annapolis, MD

Other Acts: Eilen Jewell

According to Moonalice legend, the tribe's East Coast farmers - known as preppie hippies - specialized in products for the shipping industry. Beginning in the 18th century, preppie hippies along Chesapeake Bay produced high quality rope and other hemp derivatives for the navy. Initially this meant the British Navy, but in 1775 the tribe aligned itself with the rebellion. As the first supplier of hemp products to the United States Navy, the Moonalice tribe played an unreported but legendary role in the fight for independence.

When the band arrived in Annapolis, Maryland, home of the United States Naval Academy, we immediately searched for evidence of the tribe. We didn't have to look very far. Across the street from our hotel was a deli. Hardwood and Chubby Wombat were there in search of refreshing beverages when they made a remarkable discovery. It was in the refrigerator section: Hempmilk! The label called it a "creamy non-dairy beverage made from whole hemp nuts." Milk from nuts? It makes us wonder what they call the beverage that comes from hemp udders. Housed in a purple and white one-quart package for long shelf life, the Hempmilk just begged us to buy, so we did. We took it to the gig and asked the audience for volunteers. They said it tastes like soy milk, not chicken. The band was too afraid to drink the stuff, so this will have to be the last word on the subject. For now. That said, we would point out that Hempmilk provides indisputable evidence of the evolution of the Moonalice tribe. If the Navy doesn't need rope, let the sailors drink Hempmilk!!!!

According to the Moonalice calendar (and tribal custom), attendance at gigs entitles tribal audience members to fall back on Moonalice Standard Time (MAST). The nice thing about MAST is that everyone can fall back as far as they like, as often as they like. If you are in doubt, the band recommends falling back to your 21st birthday, but that is only a guideline. If your boss gives you any flack for showing up late after a gig, just tell him or her that Chubby Wombat Moonalice said it's okay. Really.

1. Distance
2. Crazy In Heaven
3. Fair To Even Odds
4. Black Is The Color
5. I'm Glad You Think So
6. Heart Frozen Up
7. Slow Dance
8. Nick Of Time
9. Messin' With The Kid
10. Kick It Open
11. Road To Here >
12. Jumpin' Jack Flash
13. Listen To Those Eyes
14. Somebody To Love
15. Happy Endings
16. Greenport
17. Who Can Say?
18. Cynical Girl
19. Tell Me It's Okay
20. Stella Blue
21. Bleeding Of Love
22. Barbary Ellen

The Fillmore San Francisco, CA, Supporting Etta James

According to Moonalice legend, great tribal leaders go to the Happy Hemp Ground through a small number of temporal portals, which are High Holy Days in the Moonalice calendar. One of highest of these holy days is December 8. It witnessed the passing of such luminaries as Bob Bell (the original Bozo the Clown, who died in 1997), Big Walter Horton (1982), Slim Pickins (1983), and John Lennon (1980), whose contributions to the tribe are memorialized in a giant granite sculpture on Mt. Rush in Buzzville, Oregon. With Jack on the road with Hot Tuna, Moonalice 6 made its first appearance since August.

1. Distance
2. Crazy In Heaven
3. Fair To Even Odds
4. Eyesight To The Blind
5. Nick Of Time
6. Stella Blue
7. Sugaree

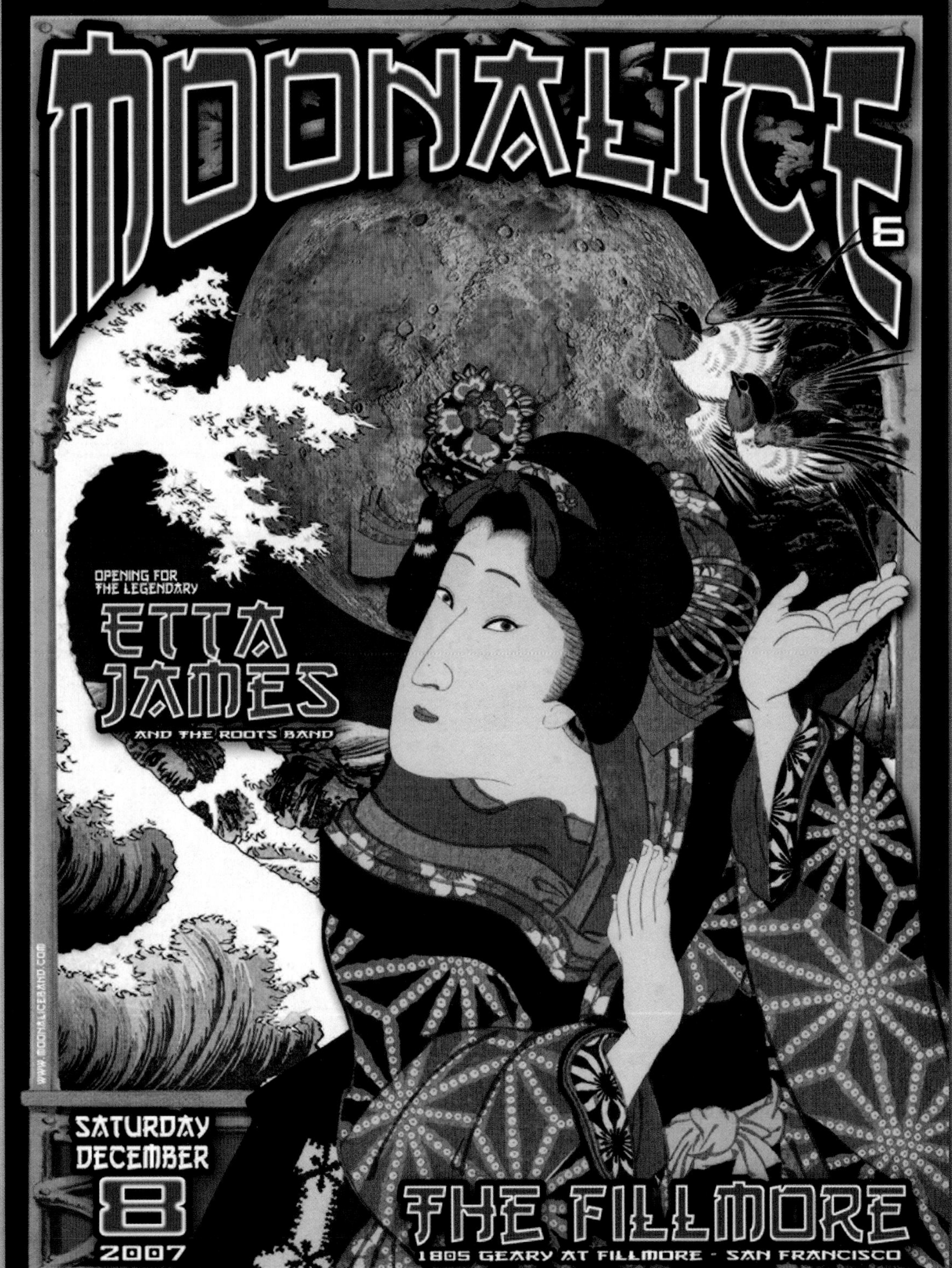

artwork by Chris Shaw

Moonalice

artwork by Chris Shaw

www.moonaliceband.com

January 8 & 9 – 2008
Wilda Marston Theatre
Loussac Library • Anchorage, Alaska

Wilda Marston Theater Anchorage, AK

According to Moonalice legend, Anchorage was the northern outpost of the Pacific hemp trade in the late 18th century. Apparently there is an untold chapter of Captain James Cook's third voyage of exploration, during which the good captain sailed north from Tahiti to Alaska. He came up the inlet to what is now Anchorage and dropped anchor. What the history books don't reveal is whether Captain Cook sold a major cargo of Tahitian hemp to the natives he met in Anchorage ... or whether the captain sampled some of the cargo himself. We believe the evidence suggests that both are correct. Why? Captain Cook, who was the finest seaman and mapmaker of his generation, mistook the inlet (which is salt water) for a river (which is fresh). Moonalice legend suggests that a captain of Cook's caliber had to be buzzed to make a mistake like that. Then Captain Cook went to Hawaii, where a different group of natives killed him for reasons that remain shrouded in the fog of history. We'll leave exploration of that part of the Legend until the band goes to Hawaii.

The band's first gig of 2008 was in a theater attached to Anchorage's city library. It was a beautiful winter evening ... almost all day long. The sun came up around 10:30 in the morning and set around 4pm. Talk about rock 'n' roll hours!

1. Whiter Shade Of Pale
2. Fair To Even Odds
3. Eyesight To The Blind
4. Crazy In Heaven
5. Silver Lining
6. Happy Endings
7. Dusty Streets Of Cairo
8. Blink Of An Eye
9. Arrowhead
10. Kick It Open
11. Distance
12. King Harvest (Has Surely Come)
13. Tell Me It's Okay
14. Listen To Those Eyes
15. Stella Blue
16. Sugaree

Wilda Marston Theater Anchorage, AK

According to Moonalice legend, January 9 was an historic day for the tribe. History shows that on January 9, 1793, a Frenchman named Jean-Pierre Blanchard attempted the first hot air balloon launch in America. The event occurred in Philadelphia and it was an A-list party. In attendance were President George Washington, Thomas Jefferson, John Adams, Henry Clay and Paul Revere, among others. The day was a huge success, as Blanchard took off, floated a mile in the air and then 15 miles downwind, landing in New Jersey.

It has been widely reported that prior to Jean-Pierre's take-off, President Washington passed something to the would-be balloonist. The history books suggest that Washington gave Blanchard a note to show people he met upon landing, just in case they thought he was from outer space. That didn't sound credible to us, so we consulted Moonalice legend. Naturally, we found the full story.

Anyone who has seen the movie National Treasure knows that Washington, Jefferson, Adams, et al were members of the Masons. What they don't know is that these patriots were also members of the Moonalice tribe. Washinton was an enormously successful hemp farmer in Virginia, and well known for the quality of his product. Moonalice legend reveals that what Washington gave Blanchard was a tightly rolled hemp product. He was reported to have said, "Yo Jean-Pierre! If you're going to be a mile high, you might as well be eight miles high! Happy landings!!"

The Sitzmark Girdwood, AK

According to Moonalice legend, altitude is positively correlated with fun. Over the centuries, tribe members have discovered many ways to gain altitude. They also discovered that combining virtual and physical altitude enhancements is a particularly powerful driver of the fun meter. Experiments in applied altitude enhancement were widely evident at the Sitzmark on this Friday night in January.

Browsing through the Moonalice legend archives, we discovered that January 11 was a momentous date in the history of the tribe. In 1913, Hudson introduced the first automobile with a hard top. Why was this introduction such a big deal? Have you ever tried to light a smoke in a fast moving convertible? Hard tops also produced a very desirable increase in back seat privacy, which led to the discovery of the drive-in and lovers' lane. Given how Hudson changed the course of civilization the company was awarded the Moonalice Prize for Changing the Course of Civilization.

1. Whiter Shade Of Pale
2. Dusty Streets Of Cairo
3. Fair To Even Odds
4. Constellation Rag
5. Crazy In Heaven
6. I'm Glad You Think So
7. Eyesight To The Blind
8. Like A Rolling Stone
9. Blink Of An Eye
10. Arrowhead
11. Kick It Open
12. Heart Frozen Up
13. Distance
14. Let It Rock
15. Tell Me It's Okay
16. Black Is The Color
17. Bleeding Of Love
18. Happy Endings
19. Stella Blue
20. Sugaree
21. Highway 61 Revisited
22. Goin' Down The Road Feeling Bad

MOONALICE

with
G.E. Smith
Pete Sears
Barry Sless
Ann McNamee
Jimmy Sanchez
Roger McNamee

artwork by Alexandra Fischer

www.moonaliceband.com

January
11th & 12th
2008

THE SITZMARK
Alyeska Resort - Girdwood, Alaska

The Sitzmark Girdwood, AK

According to Moonalice legend, January 12 is Amos and Andy Day. The original radio show began this day in 1928, with two white guys impersonating a whole lot of black people. We don't pretend to understand the significance of Amos and Andy Day, but thought we would pass it along in the interest of the Legend.

During our stay in Girdwood, we consulted a Moonalice-to-English dictionary and learned that the definition of Alyeska (in Moonalice) is "huge pile of white stuff; spending time there will get you high." We don't pretend to understand the significance of this either. That said, Girdwood is as beautiful a place as we have ever been.

1. Nick Of Time
2. Can't Hold Out
3. Crazy In Heaven
4. Fair To Even Odds
5. I Ain't Ever Satisfied
6. Greenport
7. Junko Partner
8. Listen To Those Eyes
9. Distance
10. Kick It Open
11. Whiter Shade Of Pale
12. Silver Lining
13. Barbary Ellen
14. Slow Dance
15. Somebody To Love
16. Road To Here >
17. Jumpin' Jack Flash
18. Happy Endings
19. Dusty Streets Of Cairo
20. Dance Inside The Lightning >
21. Tell Me It's Okay
22. Eyesight To The Blind
23. Stella Blue
24. Six Days on the Road
25. Sugaree

artwork by Chris Shaw

TEA LEAF GREEN

Moonalice

WED.
6
February
2008

www.moonaliceband.com

REDSTONE ROOM
at River Music Experience · 129 Main Street
Davenport, Iowa

Redstone Room Davenport, IA

Supporting Tea Leaf Green

According to Moonalice legend, it always snows in Davenport. We don't know whether it is the influence of the Big River or Highway 61, but every time we go to Davenport, the place is a hockey rink with no Zamboni. Whatever their impact in winter, the Mississippi and Highway 61 are the foundation of the long and magical musical history of Davenport. According to Wikipedia, "Davenport was founded in 1836 by Antoine LeClaire and named after his friend Colonel George Davenport after the singing of a peace treaty ending the Black Hawk War." Singing a peace treaty. What a beautiful notion. No wonder we like Davenport so much.

1. Whiter Shade Of Pale
2. Constellation Rag
3. Fair To Even Odds
4. Blink Of An Eye
5. Highway 61 Revisited
6. Road To Here >
7. Jumpin' Jack Flash

The Maintenance Shop Ames, IA

Supporting Tea Leaf Green

According to Moonalice legend, the famed ballplayer-turned-evangelist Billy Sunday was not a member of the tribe. Well, duh. Billy was committed to Prohibition, a terrible idea that runs contrary to the most fundamental beliefs of the Moonalice tribe. But Billy hailed from Ames, Iowa, which is the home of Iowa

State University and birthplace of Peter Schickele, PDQ Bach. We've never met Mr. Bach, but we've heard his music. It positively reeks of Moonalice.

Moonalice legend also holds that quality control is of paramount importance. The tribe has long believed in the power of testing its products, often at the gatherings known as gigs. In the years since the prohibition of hemp, the tribe has sought to diversify its testing services. We discovered that tribe members in Ames are part of that diversification. Ames is home to the National Animal Disease Center, where all American Mad Cow Disease samples are tested, among other things. Moonalice tribe members work with only one of those "other things." They use it make the cows happy. Everyone knows that the best way to mollify a grumpy cow is to feed her some prime hemp buds. Works every time.

The band's journey to Ames is a new chapter in the Legend . . . or a possible sequel to Spinal Tap. We left Davenport after the gig in a bus with no snow tires and a driver from Florida who didn't like winter driving. He drove onto Highway 80, went a couple miles and stopped. Black ice. The driver didn't want to go on. We pulled off the road in the lovely town of Walcott and spent the night at a Day's Inn. By the time we got to Ames – only 193 miles from Davenport – it was 3:30 the following afternoon. Tea Leaf Green, which left Davenport twelve hours after we did, arrived only five minutes behind us. It didn't matter. The Legend ruled.

1. Whiter Shade Of Pale
2. Nick Of Time
3. Greenport
4. Eyesight To The Blind
5. W.S. Walcott Medicine Show
6. Listen To Those Eyes
7. Stella Blue
8. Sugaree

TEA LEAF GREEN

MOONALICE

08-07-08

artwork by Ron Donovan

IOWA STATE UNIVERSITY
AMES-IOWA
www.moonaliceband.com

THE MAINTENANCE SHOP

103

artwork by Chris Shaw

TEA LEAF GREEN
MOONALICE

FEBRUARY 8 2008

THE CABOOZE · MINNEAPOLIS
917 CEDAR AVE SOUTH · MINNESOTA

WWW.MOONALICE.COM

Cabooze, Minneapolis, MN

Supporting Tea Leaf Green

According to Moonalice legend, size matters differently than you think. Big can be good, no question. But small has its place. History attributes the name Minneapolis to the community's first schoolteacher, who is said to have combined the Dakota word for water with the Greek word for city. Nice try. Way before the white man got to there, Moonalice tribe members inhabited the region. We consulted our trusty Moonalice-to-English dictionary and discovered that the Moonalice word "minne" actually means "small bag of hemp." Now ask yourself which explanation is more likely: City of Water or City of Small Bags of Hemp? To us, the answer is obvious.

The gig at the Cabooze added once again to Moonalice legend. In the hours before the show, Chubby Wombat came down with a stomach flu and was losing it from both ends. Fortunately, a busload of nurses from the Mayo Clinic came to the show. They administered CPR, sensual massage and all the other treatments for stomach flu. The nurses saved the day, the show went on, and went so well that the audience demanded (and got) an encore from us as the opening act. Minneapolis rules!

1. Whiter Shade Of Pale
2. I'm Glad You Think So
3. Crazy In Heaven
4. Kick It Open
5. Dusty Streets Of Cairo
6. Happy Endings
7. Somebody To Love
8. Encore: Goin' Down The Road Feeling Bad

University Center

University of Wisconsin _ Stevens Point Stevens Point, WI

Supporting Tea Leaf Green

According to Moonalice legend, George Stevens, the man who founded Stevens Point, Wisconsin was a chief in the local Moonalice tribe. Ol George was a saloon-keeper of great repute. His four saloons were the centerpiece of the town from its earliest days. George's insistence on serving whiskey by the pint was the stuff of local legend and formed the basis for the town's name. Stevens Pint didn't become Stevens Point until Prohibition reared its ugly head.

But that is only half the story. As usual, Moonalice legend has the rest. George Stevens didn't just serve whiskey. Duh. His back rooms dispensed pounds of Medical Hemp products. As any chef will tell you, "a pint's a pound the world around." The minimum quantity on offer was a pint of George's hemp, and the locals were known to hang around for days, both before and after purchase.

It was a gazillion degrees below zero in Stevens Point, but not in the University Center. Everyone there was nice and toasty!

1. Whiter Shade Of Pale
2. Empire State
3. Dubya
4. Dance Inside The Lightning
5. Who Can Say?
6. Barbary Ellen
7. Like A Rolling Stone
8. Sugaree

TEA
LEAF
GREEN

MOONALICE

FEB
9
2008

LAIRD ROOM
UNIVERSITY CENTER
1015 RESERVE ST.
STEVENS POINT · WISCONSIN

www.moonaliceband.com

artwork by Alexandra Fischer

artwork by Chris Shaw

TEN LEAF GREEN

MOONALICE

FEBRUARY 10 2008

THE RAVE-EAGLES CLUB
MILWAUKEE WISCONSIN

WWW.MOONALICEBANDS.COM

The Rave-Eagles Club Milwaukee, WI

Supporting Tea Leaf Green

According to Moonalice legend, the city of Milwaukee is located on the site of the Upper Midwest Pow wow of the Moonalice tribe, a pow wow that dates back a couple of millennia. Traditional history claims that the city got its name from either the Algonquin ("Good Land"), the Pottawotami ("Place Near Water"), or the Ojibwe ("Pleasant Land"), but Moonalice legend knows better. Way better. In Moonalice, the word "Milwaukee" means, "beer is better with hemp." To the surprise of no one, the audience confirmed the Legend.

The temperatures in the upper Midwest this week have been at or below zero … before wind chill. No matter. The exclamation point on a great evening in Milwaukee came when TLG's Trevor Garrod and Josh Clark joined us on stage for Goin' Down The Road Feeling Bad.

1. Whiter Shade Of Pale
2. Fair To Even Odds
3. Constellation Rag
4. Eyesight To The Blind
5. Crazy In Heaven
6. Arrowhead
7. King Harvest (Has Surely Come)
8. Tell Me It's Okay
9. Encore: Goin' Down The Road Feeling Bad*

*with Trevor Garrod and Josh Clark

artwork by Chris Shaw

mars area
moonalice

the ark
5.12.08
316 SOUTH MAIN STREET • ANN ARBOR • MICHIGAN
WWW.MOONALICEBAND.COM

The Ark Ann Arbor, MI

Supporting Tea Leaf Green

According to Moonalice legend, most snow in Michigan falls when the temperature is above zero degrees Fahrenheit. While this may not be the most insightful assertion in the Legend, it has certainly stood the test of time. It also proved to be correct during the band's visit to Ann Arbor, when the mercury was solidly in plus territory for the first time on this tour. As a result, heavy snow felt like a blessing!

According to local legend, Ann Arbor was founded by two land speculators, who named the town for their wives. Given that both wives were named "Ann" and neither was named "Arbor," we fail to see how you can say the town was named for them. One of the speculators built a sawmill on the site. Local Native Americans saw the mill and said "Kaw Goosh Kaw Nick! Kaw Goosh Kaw Nick!" (We're not making this up; it's in Wikipedia.) This is where local legend breaks down and Moonalice legend takes over. The locals thought the Native Americans were mimicking the sound of the sawmill. Moonalice legend knows better. In Moonalice, Kaw Goosh Kaw Nick means, "only a white man would saw lumber instead of growing hemp or playing bass!"

TLG's Reed Mathis requested and then played bass on People's Parties.

1. Whiter Shade Of Pale
2. Fair To Even Odds
3. Nick Of Time
4. Dusty Streets Of Cairo
5. Crazy In Heaven
6. W.S. Walcott Medicine Show
7. People's Parties*

*with Reed Mathis

20th Century Theater Cincinnati, OH

Supporting Tea Leaf Green

According to Moonalice legend, the waters of the Licking River near Cincinnati in southern Ohio can make anything float, even soap. Upon such small advantages are great fortunes built. History tells us that a surveyor originally called the place that is now Cincinnati, "Losantiville." They claim Losantiville combines bits of Greek, Roman, French, and English to create a word that means "City on the mouth of the Licking River." The Legend cannot argue with the mouth of the Licking. That's what mouths are for. At least that's one of the things mouths are for.

1. Whiter Shade Of Pale
2. Blink Of An Eye
3. Distance
4. Junko Partner
5. Kick It Open
6. Happy Endings
7. Listen To Those Eyes
8. Somebody To Love

THE DEAD GREEN

MOON ALICE
WEDNESDAY · FEBRUARY 13 · 2008
20th CENTURY THEATER
3021 MADISON ROAD · CINCINNATI · OHIO

One NIGHT ONLY! • "LIVE" In Concert!

Bring Your Valentine!

Stereo

Tea Leaf Green

thurs. **Feb. 14th** 20 08 **Moonalice**

www.moonaliceband.com ©2008 moonalice/rondonovan • #046 • artwork: ron donovan • printing: www.pqprint.com

artwork by Ron Donovan

House of Crave ★ 391 Neil Avenue in beautiful Columbus, Ohio • USA

114

House Of Crave Columbus, OH

Supporting Tea Leaf Green

According to Moonalice legend, February 14 is one of three hundred sixty-five High Holy Days of the tribal calendar. Among those elevated days, however, February 14 is one of the Most High. In tribal tradition, it is a day for sharing music, hemp products, and hormonal urges among lovers. While there are no tribal rules on the matter, tradition holds that the day generally featured one-on-one, rather than team activities. In some parts of the tribe, it is known as Tee Hee in the Teepee Day.

1. Whiter Shade Of Pale
2. Crazy In Heaven
3. I'm Glad You Think So
4. Empire State
5. Slow Dance
6. Fair To Even Odds
7. Arrowhead
8. Tell Me It's Okay

TEA LEAF GREEN

Moonalice.

artwork by Alexandra Fischer

FEBRUARY 15, 2008
The Music Mill
3720 EAST 82nd STREET
INDIANAPOLIS • INDIANA

www.moonaliceband.com

The Music Mill, Indianapolis, IN

Supporting Tea Leaf Green

According to Moonalice legend, Indianapolis is near the harmonic center of the tribal universe. If you find that hard to believe, take a number, but believe it. A deep bass groove emanates from the place. It permeates everything. No hills. No dales. Just a deep groove. You don't believe us? Trust the Legend.

Today we sent a big birthday shout out to Simpsons' creator Matt Groening and to the leader of the Second American Revolution, Susan B. Anthony. If it was your birthday too yeah!, we hope you had a great one.

1. Whiter Shade Of Pale
2. Constellation Rag
3. Greenport
4. Arrowhead
5. Bleeding Of Love
6. Distance
7. Stella Blue
8. Sugaree

Park West, Chicago, IL

Supporting Tea Leaf Green

According to Moonalice legend, tribal bands have frequented the Chicago area since the beginning of time. Chicago's central location was a factor, but the Legend also speaks loudly about the local hemp. If you don't believe us, look it up in Wikipedia. The name "Chicago" turns out to be the French rendering of the Miami-Illinois word "shikaakwa," which metaphorically meant "onions" or "wild leeks." The literal translation of shikaakwa was "striped skunk." We're not making this up. If "striped skunk" is not a reference to the local hemp, then Anna Nicole Smith is not a dead blonde.

Twenty-eight years ago today, in what qualifies as the prehistoric days of the modern Moonalice tribe, Chubby Wombat and Blue went out on their first date. According to Moonalice legend, the Jerry Garcia Band was playing at the University of New Haven gym. In the set list that night was Chuck Berry's Let It Rock, which, by some amazing coincidence was in the Moonalice set list for tonight.

An explosion of hormones has caused memories of February 16, 1980 to be sketchy, but both parties recall that it was the beginning of something amazing. Both Chubby and Blue remember the air freshener in the UNH gym as overpowering, which may have contributed to a loss of detail, consciousness, etc.

The ten-show Whiter Shade of Frostbite tour concluded in Chicago's Park West with Moonalice and Tea Leaf Green on stage together for Goin' Down the Road Feeling Bad, with a chorus of 400 audience members shredding their vocal chords. Huge thanks to TLG and its wonderful crew for a great tour.

1. Whiter Shade Of Pale
2. Fair To Even Odds
3. Nick Of Time
4. Let It Rock
5. Crazy In Heaven
6. Kick It Open
7. Happy Endings
8. Sugaree
9. Encore: Goin' Down the Road Feeling Bad*

*with Tea Leaf Green

TEA LEAF GREEN
MOONALICE[6]
PARK WEST ~ CHICAGO ~ 16 FEB 2008

M47 © 2008 David Singer & Moonalice · Design: DSinger · Printing: PsPrint.com

www.moonaliceband.com

artwork by Chris Shaw

Tea Leaf Green

Moonalice

February **29** 2008

The Fillmore
1805 Geary at Fillmore • San Francisco

©2008 Chris Shaw & Moonalice #040   Artwork: Chris Shaw   Printing: www.PoPrint.com

www.moonaliceband.com

Rex Foundation Benefit The Fillmore, San Francisco, CA

Supporting Tea Leaf Green

According to Moonalice legend, February 29 is the least frequent of all High Holy Days in the Moonalice calendar. The tribe calls it Leap Day, but we discovered that the official name is "Bissextile Day." Say that out loud. If it doesn't sound like a concept invented in our lovely city by the bay, then we're not bass players.

The Rex Foundation was established by Jerry Garcia and the Grateful Dead to provide money to charities and artists who can make small amounts of money go a long way. Rex practices grass roots philanthropy at its best. You can't get more Moonalice than that.

1. Whiter Shade Of Pale
2. Fair To Even Odds
3. Arrowhead
4. Crazy In Heaven
5. Tell Me It's Okay
6. Listen To Those Eyes
7. Stella Blue
8. Sugaree

artwork by Chris Shaw

MONALICE

1st
MARCH
SATURDAY
www.monaliceband.com
MOE'S ALLEY · SANTA CRUZ · CA

Moe's Alley Santa Cruz, CA

According to Moonalice legend, Bissextile Day – or Leap Day, as it is known to the tribe – is too high a holy day to last only 24 hours every four years. The ceremonies typically spill over to March 1, which turns out to be a high holy day of another kind – Beer Day! Tribal cousins who live in Iceland report that their country re-legalized beer on March 1, 1989 and now celebrates the anniversary. March 1 also happens to be the anniversary of the first day of the Salem Witch Trials, a miscarriage of justice that has been a burr under the saddle of Moonalice tribe members for nearly four hundred years. If you're having trouble keeping all this straight, you should have been with us at Moe's Alley, because it all made sense there.

1. Whiter Shade Of Pale
2. Fair To Even Odds
3. Constellation Rag
4. Buffalo Skinners
5. Crazy In Heaven
6. Fattening Frogs for Snakes
7. Like A Rolling Stone
8. Blink Of An Eye
9. Who Can Say?
10. Nick Of Time
11. Eyesight To The Blind
12. Bleeding Of Love
13. Silver Lining
14. Arrowhead
15. Greenport
16. Barbary Ellen
17. Tell Me It's Okay
18. Stella Blue
19. Junko Partner
20. Road To Here >
21. Goin' Down the Road Feeling Bad
22. Dink's Blues
23. Encore: Sugaree

The Jewish Mother (7) Virginia Beach, VA

According to Moonalice legend, the tribe demonstrated a preference for matriarchal leadership somewhere soon after the dawn of time. Within agricultural Moonalice families, it was common to entomb Moonmama in a burial mound with her most prized possession. The mounds were quite tall, owing to the fact that for many Moonmamas the prized possession was a ceremonial bong, which had to be buried upright to avoid spilling bong water into the afterlife. We bring this up because Virginia Beach is home to Mount Trashmore, an 800-foot long, 60-foot high mound reportedly built from fill. Given those dimensions, to say nothing of the prominent role of hemp in the history of the commonwealth of Virginia, we did a little investigation. The investigation was successful, but we're not tellin'. What happens in Virginia Beach stays in Virginia Beach.

Among the many great people born in Virginia Beach was Grace Sherwood, the witch of Pungo. Fortunately, her name was cleared 300 years ago. Had it not been, we would have done the job ourselves.

If D-minor is the saddest key in music, April 15 has to be the saddest day in America. Not only does everyone feel the bite of tax filing, but history has dropped some really ugly events on April 15. President Lincoln died in 1865. The Titanic sank in 1912. Wikipedia said Jason Alexander died today, so we played the show for him. It turns out Wikipedia was wrong, which is a relief, especially for Jason. The Moonalice angle on April 15 comes from ancient Latvia, where Tipsa Diena is a day to celebrate the ploughing of fields. In modern times, Tipsa Diena is just another day to get ploughed.

1. Barbary Ellen
2. Fair To Even Odds
3. Crazy In Heaven
4. Constellation Rag
5. Eyesight To The Blind
6. Listen To Those Eyes
7. Like A Rolling Stone
8. Messin' With The Kid
9. Slow Dance
10. Kick It Open
11. Dusty Streets Of Cairo
12. Greenport
13. Nick Of Time
14. Distance
15. Dance Inside The Lightning
16. Somebody To Love
17. Stella Blue
18. Arrowhead
19. Bleeding Of Love
20. Happy Endings
21. Who Can Say?
22. Junko Partner
23. Tell Me It's Okay
24. Sugaree
25. Encore: Goin' Down The Road Feeling Bad

MOONALICE

artwork by Chris Shaw

TUESDAY
FIFTEEN
APRIL
2008

THE JEWISH MOTHER
31ST AND PACIFIC AVE
VIRGINIA BEACH • VIRGINIA

Moonalice

APRIL 16th - 2008
THE 8x10
10 East Cross Street
BALTIMORE
MARYLAND

www.moonaliceband.com

The 8x10 (7) *Baltimore, MD*

According to Moonalice legend, the city of Baltimore now occupies the site of the ancient Middle Atlantic Pow Wow of the Moonalice tribe. That pow wow was known for the prodigious amounts of hemp consumed over the course of a long weekend. Remarkably, one artifact has survived from the period and the city has camouflaged it as a monument to the military-industrial complex of the 19th century. The Phoenix Shot Tower is 215 feet tall and looks like the world's tallest bong, which is what it was before the locals converted it to the production of cannon balls. What a waste.

April 16 turns out to be the saint's day for St. Bernadette, the patron saint of Motown. She was also the woman whose hallucinations in 1858 put Lourdes on the map. Could it be a coincidence that exactly 85 years later, on April 16, 1943, Dr. Albert Hofmann discovered the psychedelic effects of LSD? You be the judge. If you're not sure, just take half.

1. Nick Of Time
2. Crazy In Heaven
3. Fair To Even Odds
4. Heart Frozen Up
5. Listen To Those Eyes
6. Fattening Frogs For Snakes
7. Can't Help But Wonder Where I'm Bound
8. Barbary Ellen
9. I'm Glad You Think So
10. Blink Of An Eye
11. Kick It Open
12. Dusty Streets Of Cairo
13. Road To Here >
14. Jumpin' Jack Flash
15. Greenport
16. Somebody To Love
17. Distance
18. Dance Inside The Lightning
19. Who Can Say?
20. Arrowhead
21. Bleeding Of Love
22. Like A Rolling Stone
23. Stella Blue
24. You Can't Lose What You Never Had
25. Tell Me It's Okay
26. Let It Rock

Sellersville Theater (7) Sellersville, PA

Other Acts: Bob Malone

According to Moonalice legend, George Washington was the biggest hemp farmer in northern Virginia. Hemp was a strategic crop in those days and high profile farmers like Washington had a very personal relationship with customers. In George's case, customers signaled their need for supplies by putting up a sign that read, "George Washington slept here." While hemp's role in the economy is different today, customers still find that "George Washington slept here" signs are an effective way to indicate a need for re-supply.

Given the size of Washington's sales territory – it ran from Virginia to Connecticut – several towns emerged as distribution hubs. Sellersville, PA was one of these towns. Some have suggested it may have been the eBay of hemp in the 18th century. We don't know.

Upon arrival in Sellersville we went in search of evidence of Moonalice presence in the region. Our suspicions immediately fell on the Washington House hotel. It had the customary landmark status and a couple of historical markers out front. But no "George Washington slept here." We found this odd, as the hotel's claim to fame is that Washington really did sleep there. The lack of sign meant one of two things: either the hotel is owned by people who are not yet members of the tribe or they already have all the hemp they need, thanks. We'd like to think it's the latter.

1. Barbary Ellen
2. Fair To Even Odds
3. Crazy In Heaven
4. Eyesight To The Blind
5. Constellation Rag
6. Blink Of An Eye
7. Kick It Open
8. Arrowhead
9. Happy Endings
10. Dance Inside The Lightning
11. Distance
12. Highway 61 Revisited
13. Bleeding Of Love
14. Stella Blue
15. Sugaree
16. Encore: Like A Rolling Stone

Moonalice in Concert

At the
Sellersville Theater
Pennsylvania
17 APRIL 2008

artwork by David Singer

www.moonalice.com

129

Mr. Smalls Funhouse (7) Millvale, PA

Other Acts: Ekoostik Hookah

According to Moonalice legend, the three rivers region of western Pennsylvania has always been a hotbed of Moonalice tribal activity. The evidence has been obscured by the sands of time, but little signs are everywhere. Take the names of the rivers: Allegheny, Monongahela, and Ohio. We consulted our handy Indian-to-Moonalice dictionary and discovered that Allegheny is the Moonalice word for "thank God it's Friday!" Monongahela means "river where steel workers prefer hemp." And then there's the third river, the Ohio. Read between the "o"s. Need we say more? If rivers could have a harmonic convergence, Pittsburgh would have to be its epicenter.

People have been fighting over Pittsburgh for centuries, starting with the French and Indian Wars. Who did the English send to settle things down? Colonel George Washington. That's right, they sent Virginia's numero uno hemp farmer. Needless to say, ol George took care of the problem. History is vague about his methods, but the Legend knows … and it's not telling.

Our show in Pittsburgh was at the Legendary Mr. Smalls Funhouse, an ex-church that simply reeks of Moonalice tribal activity. We shared the stage with the amazing and wonderful Ekoostik Hookah.

1. Nick Of Time
2. Fair To Even Odds
3. Fattening Frogs for Snakes
4. Crazy In Heaven
5. Arrowhead
6. Kick It Open
7. Eyesight To The Blind
8. Bleeding Of Love
9. Somebody To Love
10. Stella Blue
11. Tell Me It's Okay

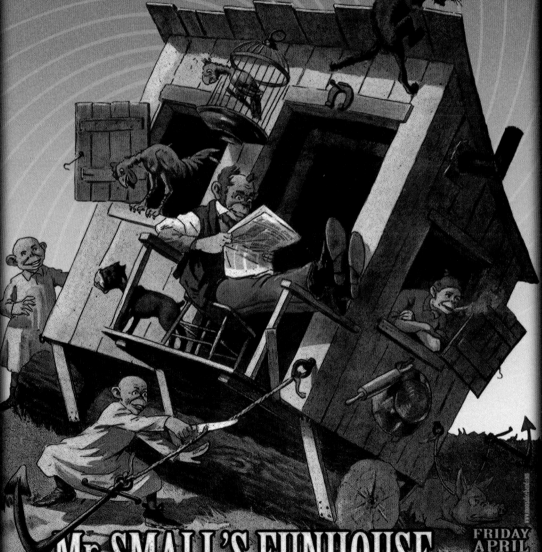

MOONALICE EKOOSTIK HOOKAH

Mr. SMALL'S FUNHOUSE
MILLVALE · PENNSYLVANIA

FRIDAY APRIL 18 2008

www.moonalice-band.com

TEA LEAF GREEN

MOONALICE

SATURDAY
APRIL 19
2008

HIGHLINE BALLROOM
NEW YORK - NEW YORK

©2008 CHRIS SHAW & MOONALICE #M54   ARTWORK: CHRIS SHAW   PRINTING: WWW.PSPRINT.COM   JOIN THE TRIBE! HTTP://WWW.MOONALICEBAND.COM

Highline Ballroom (7) New York, NY

Supporting Tea Leaf Green

According to Moonalice legend, Manhattan Island has been a major center of tribal activity going back a millennium or two. Of course Moonalice was but one of many tribes that inhabited the New York area, but the records of Moonalice influence are widespread. The conventional translation of Manhattan from the Lenape language is "island of many hills," but Wikipedia and the Encyclopedia of New York both suggest a range of more likely alternatives. Our favorite comes from the Munsee dialect of Lenape, where the word manahachtanienk means "place of general inebriation." This is consistent with the Moonalice translation of Manhattan, "place where prodigious amounts of hemp are consumed." We would also point out that the original European settlers in New York were Dutch. They called the place New Amsterdam, suggesting that they understood the value of hemp. Is it possible that the current Dutch enthusiasm for hemp products originated in the New World, rather than the other way round? Do you really need to ask?

We note that April 19 is Bicycle Day. We're not making this up. On April 19, 1943, Dr. Albert Hofmann did his first experiment with LSD. He took 250 milligrams, after which he had some difficulty speaking, so he asked his colleague to escort him home on a bicycle. That's when things got really interesting. Having survived a few hours of terror, Dr. Hofmann began to experience feelings of "good fortune and gratitude." He started to enjoy the hallucinations. He noticed that sounds had visual manifestations. He hung out for hours, feeling very good about life. Eventually, he fell asleep.

While the relationship of Bicycle Day to Moonalice or New York City eludes us, the anecdote explains the enthusiasm in some communities for April 19. But wait! There's more!!! On this date in 1927, Mae West was sentenced to 10 days in jail for obscenity in a play called, "Sex." Imagine that. Exactly a year later, the 125th and final installment of the Oxford English Dictionary was published. And this year, Moonalice and Tea Leaf Green played at the Highline.

1. Barbary Ellen
2. Fair To Even Odds
3. Crazy In Heaven
4. Constellation Rag
5. '52 Vincent Black Lightning
6. Stella Blue
7. Bleeding Of Love
8. Tell Me It's Okay
9. Sugaree

Compliments of

Moonalice

Toad's Place (7) New Haven, CT

Supporting Tea Leaf Green

According to Moonalice legend, the tribe celebrated the coming of spring each year with a day of spiritual awakening and hemp products. It was the highest of high holy days in the Moonalice calendar. In ancient times, the celebration began at dawn on April 20 and lasted as long as the participants could remain standing. In modern times, the 420 celebration typically features live music. In addition, true believers observe daily rituals without music, such as a collective inhaling of breath at 4:20 p.m.

Consider today's date. Look at the numbers . . . April 20, 2008. 4-20-08. 04-20-2008. Do you see the patterns? $4 \times 2 = 8$. $4+2+2=8$. 4-squared divided by $2=8$. There's some kind of conspiracy at work here. Probably related to the Bermuda Triangle or the disappearance of Judge Crater.

1. Whiter Shade Of Pale
2. Fair To Even Odds
3. Nick Of Time
4. Blink Of An Eye
5. Kick It Open
6. '52 Vincent Black Lightning
7. Tell Me It's Okay
8. Arrowhead
9. Sugaree

TLG420 GENADM G44 173 COMP TLG420
EVENT CODE $ 0.00 RAIN OR SHINE ADMISSION 0.00 2107215
CN 13032
GENADM
CA 84X
G44 173
TLG420

TEA LEAF GREEN
MOONALICE
TOADS PLACE
NEW HAVEN, CONNECTICUT
SUN APRIL 20 2008

SEC. GENADM
TLG420
ROW G44
C 0.00
173

TEA LEAF GREEN

MOONALICE

TOAD'S PLACE

SUN 4 20 2008

NEW HAVEN

CONNECTICUT

JOIN THE TRIBE! HTTP://WWW.MOONALICEBAND.COM

artwork by Chris Shaw

Revolution Hall (7) Troy, NY

Supporting Tea Leaf Green

According to Moonalice legend, the city of Troy, New York has long been a bastion of progressive tribal activity. We checked Wikipedia and discovered that Moonalice tribe members in Troy showed great leadership during Prohibition, becoming a "way station" for illegal alcohol going to New York City from Canada. Thanks to this infrastructure, Troy was able to diversify, complementing its speakeasies with brothels to serve western New England. Wikipedia is silent about Troy's hemp trade in those days, but it's worth noting that Troy's high profile ended with World War II, the same time that hemp prohibition took hold in the United States. Coincidence? We think not.

Today is the 26th anniversary of the Conch Republic, an outpost of the Moonalice tribe in the southeast. The Republic is the town formerly known as Key West. The town seceded from the US in 1982 to protest Border Patrol roadblocks – searching for drugs and illegal immigrants – which greatly inconvenienced residents. The Conchs declared war, surrendered a minute later, and immediately applied for $1 billion in foreign aid.

In September 1995, a Public Affairs battalion of the US Army Reserve staged an exercise in the Conch Republic ... the mission was to capture a foreign island. The Army sent PR guys to invade an island? Wow. That sounds serious! It was only an exercise, so the Army forgot to tell the Conchs, who thought they were under attack. Armed with fireboat water cannons and stale Cuban bread, the Conchs defended themselves before counterattacking at Fort Jefferson. The counterattack didn't work out, but the Republic lives on.

1. Nick Of Time	4. Eyesight To The Blind	7. Somebody To Love
2. Kick It Open	5. Constellation Rag	8. Stella Blue
3. Blink Of An Eye	6. Bleeding Of Love	9. Tell Me It's Okay

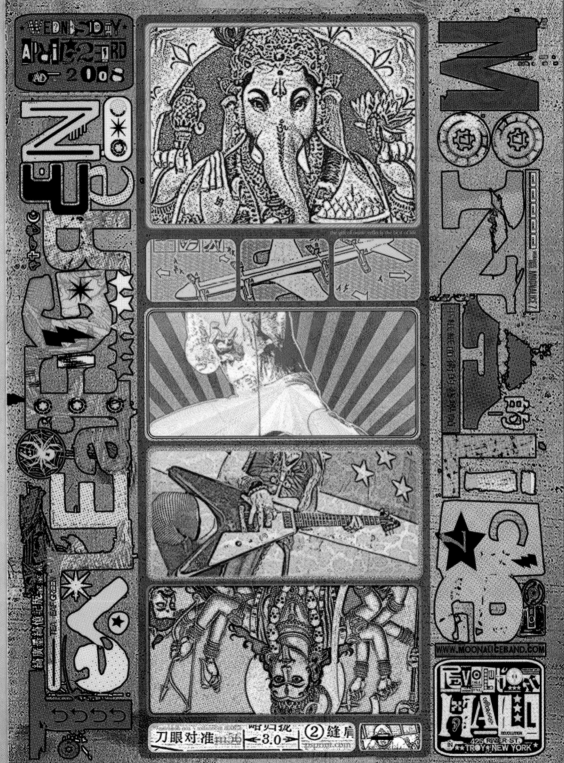

WEDNESDAY APRIL 23RD AD 2008

WWW.MOONALICEBAND.COM

425 RIVER ST.
TROY NEW YORK

TEA LEAF GREEN

MOONALICE

THURSDAY
APRIL
24
2008

HIGH FIDELITY
ROCHESTER NEW YORK
JOIN THE TRIBE! HTTP://WWW.MOONALICEBAND.COM

artwork by Chris Shaw

140

High Fidelity (7) Rochester, NY

Supporting Tea Leaf Green

According to Moonalice legend, Rochester, NY was a major center of Moonalice culture in the years before the white man came. From what we could see, the tribe is still prominent in Rochester. Around the corner from our hotel was Stone Street Cafe. A few blocks away, we found a huge sign on an overpass: Welcome to High Falls. We felt right at home.

Rochester is home to some amazing people. Susan B. Anthony was born here. Frederick Douglass lived here. Emma Goldman, Cab Calloway, Philip Seymour Hoffman, John Lithgow, Chuck Mangione, Ol Hoss Radbourne, Mitch Miller, and Gorilla Monsoon all hail from Rochester. But our favorite Rochester natives are the Fox sisters, Kate, Leah, and Margaret. They were spiritualists in the 19th century. In their presence, people could communicate with the dead. Their séances attracted the best and brightest of the time, including James Fenimore Cooper, Horace Greeley, and William Lloyd Garrison. For 40 years the Fox sisters were a phenomenon. Then they got mad at each other and one of the sisters blew the whistle. They had faked it from the word go. Bummer.

1. Nick Of Time
2. Fair To Even Odds
3. Crazy In Heaven
4. I Can't Stand Up
5. Slow Dance
6. Empire State
7. Dusty Streets
8. Kick It Open
9. Tell Me It's Okay

Higher Ground (7) Burlington, VT

Supporting Tea Leaf Green

According to Moonalice legend, Vermont has magical powers.

Burlington is the biggest city in Vermont and one of the few known habitats of the Moonalice tribe's nomadic clan. It has always had great music. Now it also produces really good ice cream. And snowboards. And craft beer. And chocolate. And bagels. In short, Burlington is heaven. Burlington also gave us Orson Bean, Howard Dean, Patrick Leahy, Harry Bliss, and 75% of Phish. Pretty cool.

April 25 is a big day in history. Our favorite fun facts . . . In 1961, Robert Noyce was granted a patent for the integrated circuit. Eight years earlier – on April 25, 1953 – Watson and Crick published their first paper on DNA.

1. Barbary Ellen >
2. Nick Of Time
3. Crazy In Heaven
4. Fair To Even Odds
5. Dusty Streets Of Cairo
6. Blink Of An Eye
7. Distance
8. Kick It Open
9. Bleeding Of Love
10. Tell Me It's Okay

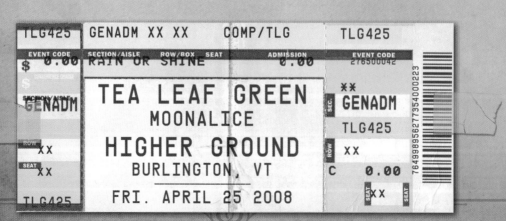

TEA LEAF GREEN

higher·ground
BURLINGTON · VT
4.25.08
www.moonaliceband.com

MOONALICE

The Paradise (7) Boston, MA

Supporting Tea Leaf Green

According to Moonalice legend, the tribe fled Boston in the early 19th century. This departure, long unexplained, is notable because Boston had long been a major center for the Moonalice tribe, which played a huge role at the Boston Tea Party (see Moonalice History for Nov 1, 2007) and Bunker Hill. Then they all hit the road, beginning in 1820. No one knew why . . . until now.

The band did some research and discovered a likely explanation for the tribal exodus: the leveling of Beacon Hill. Anyone who has spent time in Boston recently knows that Beacon Hill features a whole lot of expensive real estate, but not much elevation. This was not always the case. There used to be a real hill there until the city decided to use the dirt of Beacon Hill to fill in the marshes of what is now HaymarketSquare. What the city fathers did not realize at the time was that Beacon Hill was way more than a hill. It was a Moonalice burial mound. (For an explanation of Moonalice burial mounds, see the History for April 15, 2008). The Moonmothers of ancient Boston had mighty big bongs, which accounted for the height of the Hill. The tribe was so thoroughly dismayed by the city's wanton disregard for Moonalice heritage that it abandoned the area for nearly 200 years. It turns out that the tribe didn't stay away because of unresolved emotional issues. Nope. The explanation is much simpler. The tribe sampled so much of its own crop that it just forgot to go back. We hate it when that happens.

So Moonalice (the band) returned to Boston this day for its second visit in four months. It was the last show of a ten-show run with Jack and we celebrated with an extra helping of Howling Monkey. Yowzah! We may never come down!!! …

TEA LEAF GREEN
MOONALICE 7

THE PARADISE · BOSTON

26 April 2008

artwork by David Singer

By the way, the National Weather service reports that the odds of an individual being struck by lightning over the course of an 80-year life are 1 in 3,000. The probability of being struck twice in a lifetime is 1 in 9 million. Ignoring the odds, we played two different "Lightning" songs in the same night. Who says music can't beat the odds?

1. Whiter Shade Of Pale
2. I'm Glad You Think So
3. '52 Vincent Black Lightning
4. Distance
5. Love In Vain >
6. Stella Blue
7. Dance Inside The Lightning >
8. Tell Me It's Okay
9. Sugaree

Neighborhood Theatre Charlotte, NC

Supporting Tea Leaf Green

According to Moonalice legend, the ancient tribe struggled to survive in the Piedmont region of North Carolina. Then sometime in the 18th century, they went their own way and contact was lost with other Moonalice families. We learned the full story in Charlotte from Tar Heel Moonalice, matriarch of the tribe in North Carolina. It turns out that the Piedmont climate was unsuitable for hemp farming, but too nice to abandon. And so the local tribe diversified into other crops: tobacco and corn likker. Tobacco lacked the versatility of hemp, but was addictive even for politicians and judges, which helped to keep it legal. According to Chief Tar Heel, tobacco supported the tribe economically while bootlegging provided much needed exercise. The local tribe members raced their product around in cars souped up to outrun tax collectors and police. This eventually led to stock car racing. Which means NASCAR descended from bootlegging, which descended from Moonalice! How cool is that? Of course, the tribe called their beverage, "Moonshine."

1. Sugaree
2. Constellation Rag
3. Crazy In Heaven
4. Fair To Even Odds
5. I Can't Stand Up
6. Kick It Open
7. Bleeding Of Love
8. Eyesight To The Blind
9. Tell Me It's Okay

TEA LEAF GREEN

MOONALICE

NEIGHBORHOOD THEATER

MAY DAY

5·1·08

CHARLOTTE · NORTH CAROLINA

artwork by Chris Shaw

JOIN THE UNION! HTTP://WWW.MOONALICE.COM

147

The Pour House Charleston, SC

Supporting Tea Leaf Green

According to Moonalice legend, Charleston was a major hub of tribal trading in the 18th century, when the American Revolution began. When the British imposed the Tea Act on the colonies in 1773, two towns rebelled. Everyone knows the story of the Boston Tea Party (Moonalice legend. 11-1-07), but the story of the Charleston Revolt remains clouded in mystery. As in Boston, the raiding was the work of Moonalice tribe members. Unlike Boston, the product they seized turned out to be hemp, which explains why they "impounded" it, rather than tossing it into the harbor. As usual, history makes much more sense through the lens of the Moonalice legend.

1. Barbary Ellen
2. Nick Of Time
3. Crazy In Heaven
4. Fair To Even Odds
5. Heart Frozen Up
6. Slow Dance
7. Happy Endings
8. Arrowhead
9. Tell Me It's Okay

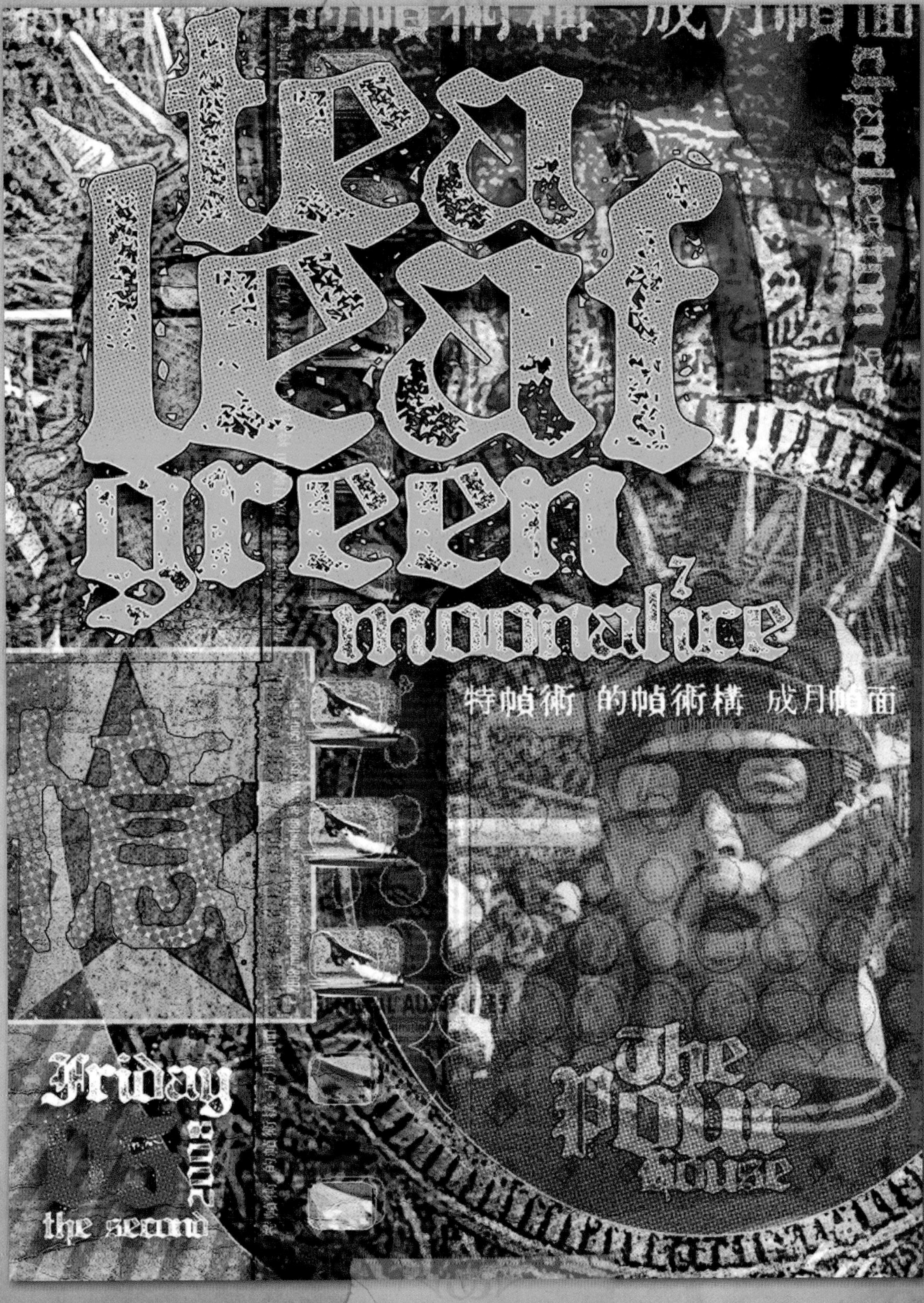

tea leaf green

moonalice

artwork by Ron Donovan

charleston sc

特帕術 的帕術構 成月帕面

friday 2008

the second

The Pour House

artwork by Alexandra Fischer

Sea Leaf Green

Moonalice

Variety Playhouse
Atlanta ~ Georgia

Saturday
May 3, 2008

Join the Tribe at www.moonalice.com

150

Variety Playhouse Atlanta, GA

Supporting Tea Leaf Green

According to Moonalice legend, the 3rd of May is Trio de Mayo, the Day of Rehearsal for the tribe. Traditionally, it was a practice day for Cinco de Mayo, with a day off in between to recover. This year, May 3 was also Gig Day in Atlanta.

While perusing the closest thing we know to the Encyclopedia Gallactica, we discovered that May 3 is also Discoflux, the fifth holiday of the Discordian calendar. Digging deeper, we learned that since 1958 there has been a Discordian religion, centered on the notion that chaos is as important as order. Wow. How could we not know about this? The Discordians' key text, the Principia Discordia, begins with the following quote:

"If organized religion is the opium of the masses, then disorganized religion smokes the marijuana of the lunatic fringe."

We couldn't have said it better ourselves. Never has a band felt more welcome at a gig than we did at the Variety Playhouse. We parked the bus in front of the theater, across the street from an apartment complex called the Bass Lodge. We hadn't realized it until now, but any place Moonalice stays is a Bass Lodge.

1. Whiter Shade Of Pale
2. Road To Here >
3. Jumpin' Jack Flash
4. Fair To Even Odds
5. Crazy In Heaven
6. Dusty Streets Of Cairo
7. Bleeding Of Love
8. Stella Blue
9. Arrowhead
10. Tell Me It's Okay

The Baby Grand, Wilmington, DE

Supporting Tea Leaf Green

According to Moonalice legend, the tribe's agricultural clan was often forced to disguise its crop to avoid confrontations with the authorities. As we discovered in Charlotte, tribe members in the Piedmont region went so far as to grow something else: tobacco. But in Mid-Atlantic States like Delaware, the tribe stuck with hemp, making subterfuge a necessity, as well as a fine art. We learned more in the 3rd inning of the Wilmington Blue Rocks game, when a mascot like no other ran onto the field: Mr. Celery. We kid you not. A stalk of celery with a goofy grin, green shorts, and green knee socks. The entire ball field could have been full of hemp and you would never have known. All eyes were on Mr. Celery.

In Atlanta, we learned about the Discordians, who believe that chaos is as worthy as order. It went from theoretical to real when we arrived in Wilmington. Across the street from our hotel was the 1st and Central Presbyterian Church. You would think the church must be at 1st and Central, right? And you would be wrong. It's at 11th and Market. This has to be the work of the Discordians.

The signs point to Moonalice culture valuing confusion more than chaos. The tribe accepts that life is uncertain and recommends enjoying it. If you don't know how, go to a minor league baseball game.

For the second time, lightning struck twice in a short set.

1. Barbary Ellen
2. Constellation Rag
3. Crazy In Heaven
4. Fair To Even Odds
5. '52 Vincent Black Lightning
6. Dance Inside The Lightning
7. Kick It Open
8. Bleeding Of Love
9. Dusty Streets Of Cairo
10. Tell Me It's Okay

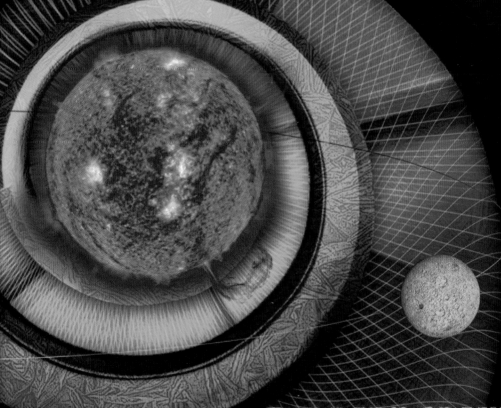

Tea Leaf Green

Moonalice

artwork by Chris Shaw

Tuesday
MAY 6
2008
JOIN THE TRIBE! www.moonaliceband.com

THE BABY GRAND
318 N. Market Street
Wilmington - Delaware

©2008 Chris Shaw & Moonalice #063 · Artwork: Chris Shaw · Printing: www.PsPrint.com

IN BEAUTIFUL NEW YORK CITY

MOON ALICE!

WEDNESDAY MAY 7TH 2008

THE REBEL

JOIN THE TRIBE AT WWW.MOONALICEBAND.COM

Jammy Awards Pre-Party Rebel, New York, NY

With Yuto Miyazawa (age 8)

According to Moonalice legend, hemp grown on Manhattan island has unique powers. Apparently it makes you incomprehensibly generous. How else do you explain the Lenape tribe selling the island for $24 in beads or the Dutch trading it for a microscopic island in Indonesia? Such acts of generosity eventually resulted in the tribe's agricultural clan being displaced and the island going "smokeless". In the process, New York became the biggest city in the country and the one with the lowest per capita carbon footprint. When the nomadic clan comes to town the locals break out their tribal air freshener, confident that they are not contributing to global warming.

This show will remain forever etched in our memory because it was the first North American performance by Yuto Miyazawa. Yuto is 8 years old. He plays a Randy Rhoades Flying V with black polka dots that is at least six inches taller than he is. But Yuto knows guitars. He played and sang Crossroads. It was unbelievable. The video is on YouTube.

1. Barbary Ellen
2. Nick Of Time
3. Crazy In Heaven
4. Fair To Even Odds
5. Eyesight To The Blind
6. Crossroads*
7. Stella Blue
8. Bleeding Of Love
9. Tell Me It's Okay
10. Sugaree

* backing Yuto Miyazawa

World Cafe Live *Philadelphia, PA*

Supporting Tea Leaf Green

According to Moonalice legend, the Philadelphia branch of the tribe organized itself as a matriarchy centuries ago. The tribe didn't know much about biology and nothing about estrogen. They just knew that putting women in charge meant less war and more hemp production. And so it was until the Revolutionary War, when a bunch of very bright young men took over. From that point on, womenfolk — as well as the entire Moonalice tribe — were on the defensive. A few brave souls in Philadelphia, beginning with Betsy Ross, stood up for the matriarchy, but few people listened until the very beginning of the 20th century. That's when Philly resident Anna Marie Jarvis lobbied successfully for a holiday on the second Sunday in May to honor the matriarchy. She called it Mothers Day and dedicated it to peace and feminism. The first Mothers Day was 100 years ago tomorrow. Unfortunately, somewhere along the way Anna Marie's values were replaced by those of Hallmark. Peace and feminism gave way to cards, chocolates, and roses. We honor Anna Marie as she honored her mom, a Moonalice chief of great repute.

1. Somebody To Love
2. Fair To Even Odds
3. Dance Inside Lightning
4. Silver Lining
5. Messin' With The Kid
6. Whiter Shade Of Pale
7. Buffalo Skinners
8. Stella Blue
9. Tell Me It's Okay

Tea Leaf Green
Moonalice

artwork by Chris Shaw

MAY 8 2008

World Cafe Live
Philadelphia - Pennsylvania

GREEN TEA

©2008 Chris Shaw & Moonalice #M04 · Artwork: Chris Shaw · Printing: www.PsPrint.com

TEA LEAF GREEN

MOONALICE

artwork by Chris Shaw

Friday • May 9 • 2008

The 8x10 • Baltimore • Maryland

The 8 x 10 Baltimore, MD

Supporting Tea Leaf Green

According to Moonalice legend, the tribe had a slang term for anything that is pure in an old school sort of way. They called it "ornithologically correct." In the context of hemp, this meant reversing centuries of genetic engineering, working from heirloom seeds, and growing plants that are vintage, if not potent. The term "ornithologically correct" has also been applied to team mascots. The Legend suggests that Mr. Celery and the Philly Phanatic are "ornithologically correct," while the plush version of the Oriole Bird is, well, you know, a cartoon character.

1. Somebody To Love
2. Fair To Even Odds
3. Dance Inside Lightning
4. Silver Lining
5. Messin' With The Kid
6. Whiter Shade Of Pale
7. Buffalo Skinners
8. Stella Blue
9. Tell Me It's Okay

*with Mookie Siegel on piano

Mr. Smalls Funhouse Millvale, PA

Supporting Tea Leaf Green

According to Moonalice legend, the tribe revered children of multiple births. Twins are special. Triplets are one and a half times as special. When there are more than three born together, the tribe stops everything and declares a regional holiday on the birthday. In Pennsylvania, the biggest Kahuna of baby holidays is for the Gosselin Sextuplets, who are – you guessed it – triply special.

Alexis, Hannah, Aaden, Collin, Leah, and Joel were christened the Hershey Kisses, on account of where they were born on May 10, 2004. This was their day; we're just lucky to be part of it.

Today is also the 136th anniversary of the nomination of the first woman to run for president. Her name was Victoria Woodhull and she was nothing short of amazing. She made a fortune on Wall Street with her sister, the first women brokers in stock exchange history. Then she dedicated herself to two propositions: women's suffrage and free love. Those of you who are experienced in the Moonalice legend can probably tell where this is going. Victoria was not popular with other leaders of the suffrage movement - such as Susan B. Anthony, who apparently had a problem with the free love part - but Vickie was REALLY popular with Moonalice tribe members. Still is. We're hoping she runs again. She can't be any older than one of the guys running for president.

Three members of Tea Leaf Green joined us on stage for the final song of this great East Coast tour. We love TLG and look forward to touring with them again soon.

1. Buffalo Skinners
2. Fair To Even Odds
3. Blink Of An Eye
4. Arrowhead
5. City of New Orleans
6. Kick It Open
7. Bleeding Of Love
8. Tell Me It's Okay
9. Sugaree*

*with Trevor Garrod, Josh Clark, and Steve Adams of Tea Leaf Green

TEA LEAF GREEN
MOONALICE

artwork by David Singer

10 May 2008

Millvale, PA

Mr. Small's Funhouse

WAVY GRAVY'S 72ND BIRTHDAY CELEBRATION

A BENEFIT FOR CAMP WINNARAINBOW FEATURING

MOONALICE
WITH SPECIAL GUESTS

MICKEY HART
AND BARRY MELTON

JONATHAN RICHMAN

DAVID NELSON

RAMBLIN' JACK ELLIOT

EMORY JOSEPH AND WOODY VERMEIRE

WAVY GRAVY AND THE CLOWN CONSPIRACY

MAY 15 2008

THE THROCKMORTON THEATER
MILL VALLEY • CALIFORNIA

artwork by Chris Shaw

JOIN THE TRIBE! www.moonaliceband.com

©2008 Chris Shaw & Moonalice #M68 • Artwork: Chris Shaw • Printing: www.PsPrint.com

Wavy Gravy's 72nd Birthday 142 Throckmorton Theatre, Mill Valley, CA

According to Moonalice legend, clowns are the social equivalent of Crazy Glue. They stand out in a crowd because of their red foam noses and very large shoes, but their commitment to adding mirth to every situation is what commands respect in the tribe. "Mirthiness" was the hallmark of the Moonalice philosopher Confusion, whose multifaceted career included a stint as master of ceremonies for the ancient festival known as Clownstock.

Like so much of Moonalice culture, Clownstock adapted to survive. Its present home is Camp Winnarainbow in Northern California, where the master of clown-emonies is Saint Misbehavin' himself, Wavy Gravy. As spiritual leader of the tribe in the Bay Area, Wavy had the honor of being the first to moon the band at a show. He also channeled the philosopher Confusion with his statement at Woodstock, "if you aren't sure, only take half."

Wavy was born this day in 1936, a birth date he shares with the great cartoonist Ralph Steadman. May 15 is also the birthday of Las Vegas (1905) and the Asylum for the Relief of Persons Deprived of the Use of Their Reason (1817), the first private mental health hospital in the United States.

One highlight of this great celebration: Ratdog guitarist Mark Karan joined us on stage for Tell Me It's Okay and Sugaree.

1. Whiter Shade Of Pale
2. Silver Lining
3. Buffalo Skinners
4. Fair To Even Odds
5. Crazy In Heaven
6. Stella Blue
7. Bleeding Of Love
8. Tell Me It's Okay*
9. Sugaree**

*with Mark Karan (lead guitar) and Woody Vermeire (fiddle).
**with Mark Karan (lead guitar), Woody Vermeire (fiddle), and Emory Joseph (vocals).

Mystic Theatre Petaluma, CA

Supporting Marshall Tucker Band

According to Moonalice legend, the Coast Miwok tribe of northern California may have held a Moonalice franchise in the years before Europeans arrived. The Miwoks had many villages in and around present day Petaluma. When the Spanish showed up with their plan to build a mission, they asked the name of the area. The Miwoks pointed at the Europeans and said, "péta lúuma." The Europeans thought the phrase meant, "hill backside." Huh? We looked for guidance in a Moonalice-English dictionary . . . "horse's backside." Ah. Those Miwoks were such kidders.

1. Whiter Shade Of Pale
2. Constellation Rag
3. Crazy In Heaven
4. Fair To Even Odds
5. Cynical Girl
6. Listen To Those Eyes
7. Blink Of An Eye
8. Dusty Streets Of Cairo
9. Tell Me It's Okay
10. Encore: Road To Here >
11. Jumpin' Jack Flash

Mystic Theater

Presents

Marshall Tucker Band
Moonalice₆

Petaluma, California ~ 16 May 2008

M69 © 2008 David Singer & Moonalice ~ Design: DSinger ~ Printing: PsPrint.com

http://www.moonaliceband.com

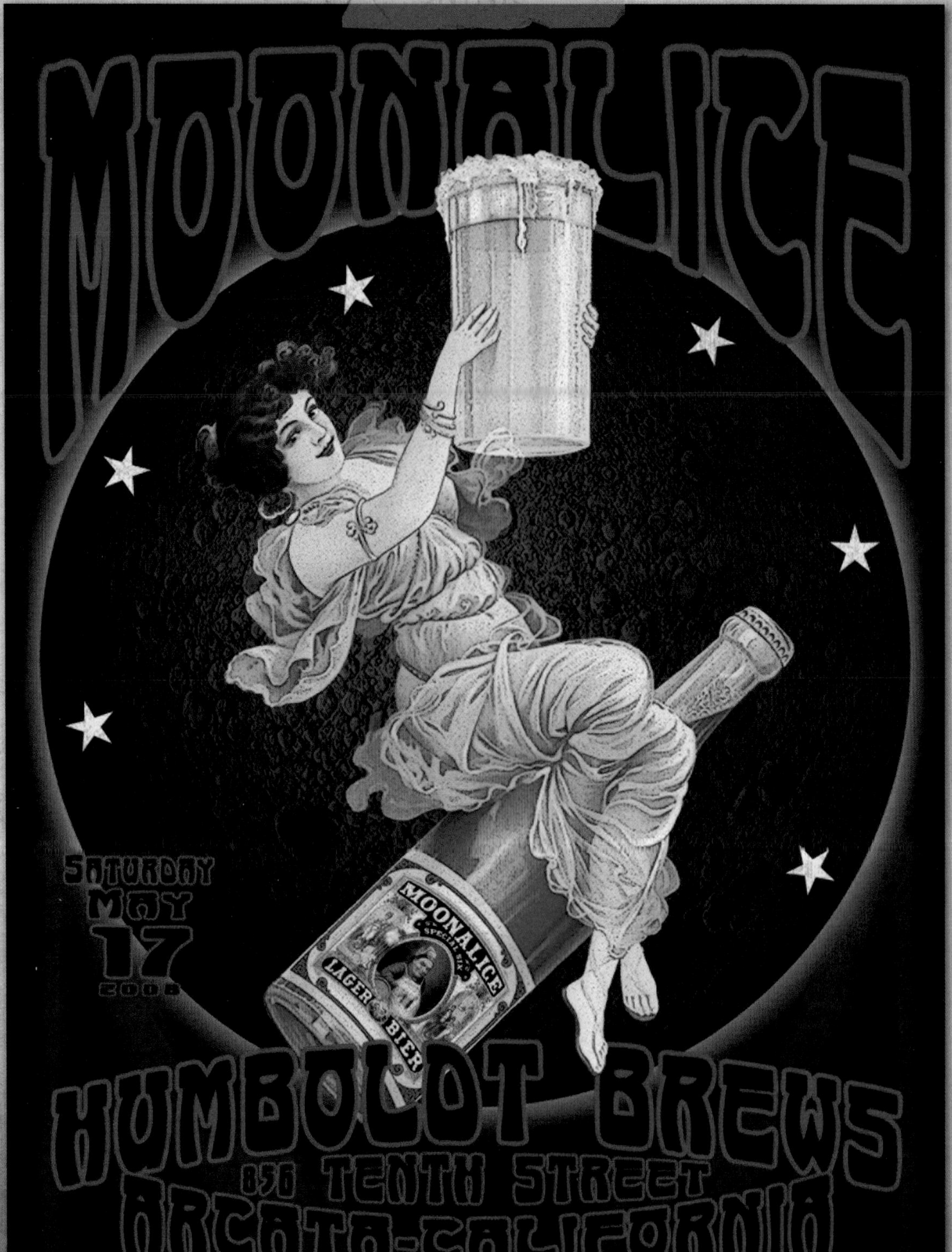

artwork by Chris Shaw

Humboldt Brews Arcata, CA

According to Moonalice legend, the Northern California coast has always had magical qualities that protect the tribe from harassment. The soil is also unusually fertile, enabling hippies to grow some of the world's finest strains of hemp. While Humboldt rope no longer enjoys huge demand from ships of sail, the tribe in the region has adjusted with a range of alternative hemp products. Hemp beer, milk, and clothing are in evidence around Arcata, as are high-end organic products based on hemp flowers.

The politics of Arcata are unusually hospitable for the tribe. In 1989, Arcata made itself a Nuclear-Free Zone. In 2003, the city was the first to make voluntary compliance with the Patriot Act illegal. While they have not been able to reverse the Prohibition of hemp, the citizens of Arcata have demonstrated a commitment to doing so. In short, it's a Moonalice kind of town.

1. Barbary Ellen
2. Fair To Even Odds
3. Constellation Rag
4. '52 Vincent Black Lightning
5. Crazy In Heaven
6. Fattening Frogs for Snakes
7. Slow Dance
8. Kick It Open
9. Nick Of Time
10. Heart Frozen Up
11. Greenport
12. I'm Glad You Think So
13. Arrowhead
14. Stella Blue
15. Whiter Shade Of Pale
16. Tell Me It's Okay
17. Encore: Dink's Blues

MOONALICE

artwork by Alexandra Fischer

SCHWAGSTOCK 37

SALEM * MISSOURI

FRIDAY & SATURDAY
MAY 23rd
24th &
2008

CAMP ZOE

Schwagstock (5) Salem, MO

According to Moonalice legend, the tribe declares a High Holy Day whenever a nomadic band plays a gig. Some High Holy Days are higher than others, but all gig days are high. May 23 is High and Holy three ways to Friday. First, it is the Day of Disunity in the Discordian calendar. (Disunity was the word of the day for Moonalice, the band, as Blue was not with us for family reasons.) Second, it is World Turtle Day. By coincidence, two large, green dancing turtles adorned the stage. One member of the audience said she was a Goffle, a person who celebrates turtles. Others in the audience did not claim to be Goffles, but were celebrating turtles in their own way, often by burning small offerings of plant material. Third, today is the saint day of Aaron the Illustrious. Aaron was a monk in the 4th century, which probably means he got to be a saint by having hallucinations. All we know is that Aaron was also known as Aaron the Nuts. We are not making this up. Aaron the Nuts. Does this refer to his hallucination? His anatomy? You be the judge.

Schwagstock is a great scene in a really cool location. We celebrated with a set that included three – count 'em THREE – bass solos by Sir Sinjin. After our set, Sir Sinjin, Jesùs H., and Chubby all joined the Schwag on stage for a rowdy rendition of Goin' Down the Road Feeling Bad.

1. Barbary Ellen
2. Fair To Even Odds
3. Constellation Rag
4. '52 Vincent Black Lightning
5. Crazy In Heaven
6. Fattening Frogs for Snakes
7. Slow Dance
8. Kick It Open
9. Nick Of Time
10. Heart Frozen Up
11. Greenport
12. I'm Glad You Think So
13. Arrowhead
14. Stella Blue
15. Whiter Shade Of Pale
16. Tell Me It's Okay
17. Encore: Dink's Blues

Schwagstock (5) Salem, MO

According to Moonalice legend, the tribe didn't really sell Manhattan Island to Peter Minuet for $24 in trinkets. They swapped it for a piece of Connecticut where hemp grew better than it did on Manhattan. The $24 in trinkets was a bonus, like in a Ginsu knife commercial. The Manhattan deal was 382 years ago today, but it seems like only yesterday.

On this day in 1820, a song called "Mary Had A Little Lamb" was published. What they don't tell you is that the song was based on a Moonalice tribal song, "Alice Had A Little White Rabbit." Legend also refers to an obscure alternative version called, "Alice Had A Little Weed, Then She Had a Little More, Then She Had the Munchies."

Happy Birthday to Tommy Chong and Bob Dylan.

1. Barbary Ellen
2. I'm Glad You Think So
3. Fair To Even Odds
4. Nadine
5. Like A Rolling Stone
6. '52 Vincent Black Lightning
7. Stella Blue
8. Junko Partner
9. Tell Me It's Okay
10. Sugaree

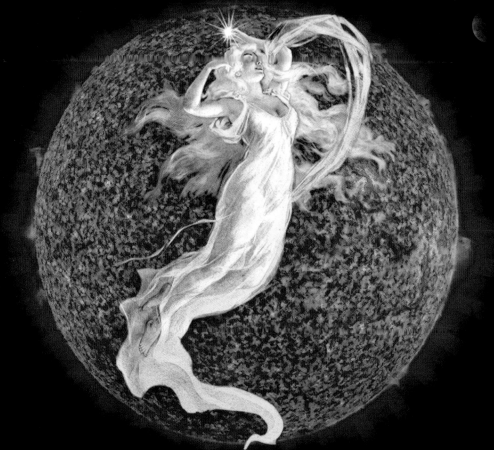

artwork by Chris Shaw

MOONALICE

SUNDAY MAY 25 2008
FESTA DI BELLA SOLE
GENEVA MINNESOTA

JOIN THE TRIBE! www.moonaliceband.com

172

Festi Di Bella Sol Geneva, MN

According to Moonalice legend, the answer to most questions is "42." Not every question, mind you, but enough to matter. You can imagine the tribe's surprise when Douglas Adams published "The Hitchhiker's Guide to the Galaxy" and declared that "42" is the answer to everything. Perhaps it is, once you get beyond the Earth's gravity. But here on earth, where Confusionism reigns, some questions have no answer. "Hey! Where'd everybody go?" is an example.

Today is Towel Day, which commemorates the life and writings of the great Mr. Adams. We took the stage, armed with a lovely red towel from the bus, and played a set where every song was connected to the one before and the one after. Some kind of Force emanated from the audience and the ring of majestic oaks that surrounded the stage. No wonder. Today is also Universal Day of the Jedi and the 31st anniversary of the release of Star Wars. Played our hearts out, we did. Great show, it was.

1. Dusty Streets Of Cairo >
2. Crazy In Heaven >
3. Kick It Open >
4. Nick Of Time >
5. Dance Inside The Lightning >
6. Legend >
7. Stella Blue >
8. Fair To Even Odds >
9. Somebody To Love >
10. Whiter Shade Of Pale >
11. Tell Me It's Okay

Bill Graham Foundation Benefit
The Fillmore @ Irving Plaza, New York, NY

Other Acts:
John Popper & Chan Kinchla, Spin Doctors, Dark Star Orchestra

According to Moonalice legend, three is a very powerful (and lucky) number. It symbolizes the bewildering trinity of sects, hemp, and low-toned music. Every Moonalice tribe member trains in the entire trinity for many years before choosing a "major" which determines the clan with which he or she will spend the rest of his or her life. Most choose to stay with the clan into which they were born, but the tribe supports those who choose a different path. Always tolerant in matters of personal choice, the tribe also supports those who choose not to. In addition, it supports those who can't make up their mind.

Whether the context is Blind Mice, Stooges, Musketeers, Wise Men, or Little Pigs, three has changed the world for the better. Why should the Moonalice legend be any different?

The band's third gig in New York City (in only six weeks) was a Bill Graham Foundation benefit at the Fillmore, née Irving Plaza. Since it opened in 1914, the venue has been home to burlesque, Yiddish theater, and Polish dance, as well as rock 'n' roll. It once saw Gypsy Rose Lee (all of her, in the Full Monty sense). It's on an island that the Moonalice tribe once swapped to Peter Minuit for $24 in trinkets and a piece of Connecticut. (Moonalice legend, 4-19-08.) Coincidently, the gig celebrated Mother's Day in Bolivia and Sweden, as well as the birthdays of Rachel Carson, Vincent Price, Harlan Ellison, and Batman.

1. Whiter Shade Of Pale
2. I Ain't Ever Satisfied
3. Crazy In Heaven
4. Stella Blue
5. Tell Me It's Okay

A BILL GRAHAM FOUNDATION BENEFIT

MOONALICE

SPIN DOCTORS · JOHN POPPER AND CHAN KINCHLA

DARK STAR ORCHESTRA

MAY 27 2008

THE FILLMORE

NEW YORK AT IRVING PLAZA

JOIN THE TRIBE www.MOONALICEBAND.COM

artwork by Chris Shaw

MOONALICE

G.E. Smith · Barry Sless · Pete Sears · Ann McNamee · Roger McNamee · Jimmy Sanchez

GVGA 2008 Annual Conference · The Best of Things

Thursday · May 29 · 2008

The Fairmont Queen Elizabeth Hotel
Montreal · Quebec

176

Private Event Fairmont Queen Elizabeth, Montreal, Quebec

According to Moonalice legend, change is good. Especially if you are a coin collector.

In Canada, today is the Day of Action for people of the First Nations. We lost the receipt for Moonalice's First Nation status, but that didn't stop us from taking action on behalf of all Canada's First Nations. Ironically, today is also Oak Apple Day in Great Britain, a day which celebrates the restoration of the British monarchy. Can't say we were excited about that until we learned that the Oak Apple ceremony may have descended from pre-Christian nature worship.

Did you know they have 20 miles of tunnels under Montreal? You could live down there if you wanted to. Especially in the winter.

1. Whiter Shade Of Pale
2. Constellation Rag
3. Fair To Even Odds
4. Crazy In Heaven
5. '52 Vince Black Lightning
6. Nick Of Time
7. Kick It Open
8. Dance Inside The Lightning
9. Sugaree

Summer Arts & Music Festival Garberville, CA

According to Moonalice legend, sacred places exist where the magical beat of Confusionism overwhelms gravity and other forces of nature. Today, Sir Sinjin led us to Confusion Hill, a roadside attraction just south of Garberville, where time fluctuates, balls and water flow uphill, and nothing is quite as you would expect. So powerful was the magic emanating from Confusion Hill that both Hardwood and Chubby felt its effects from miles away. Of course, being Confusionists they weren't sure what they were feeling.

We played today's show for Alton Kelley, one of the great artists of the 20th Century. With his partner, Stanley Mouse, Kelley was a giant in the San Francisco poster art revolution of the mid-'60s. Kelley died today and we miss him already.

1. Whiter Shade Of Pale
2. Nick Of Time
3. Fair To Even Odds
4. Danny & Laura
5. Crazy In Heaven
6. Stella Blue
7. Buffalo Skinners
8. Tell Me It's Okay
9. Sugaree

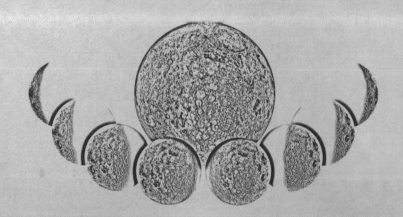

MOONALICE

artwork by Chris Shaw

SUNDAY
JUNE 1
2008

SUMMER ARTS & MUSIC FESTIVAL
BENBOW STATE RECREATION AREA
GARBERVILLE-CALIFORNIA

JOIN THE TRIBE! WWW.MOONALICEBAND.COM

Harmony Festival Santa Rosa, CA

According to Moonalice legend, pow wows associated with the spring planting season were a welcome respite from heavy labor in the fields. As Moonalice technology evolved, these pow wows turned into trade shows with the latest equipment for growers ... and lots of good music. Imagine our joy when we learned that the Harmony Festival is the modern incarnation of that pow wow. There is such vitality in the agricultural side of the Moonalice economy!

From our perch on the stage, we noted widespread evidence of last year's successful harvest in the region. The sweet smell of prosperity . . .

We read in Wikipedia that Santa Rosa has been looking for a new motto. Apparently the Luther Burbank-inspired phrase "The City Designed For Living" doesn't cut it any longer. We don't anticipate that our views will carry any weight, but we have a few modest suggestions:

- Santa Rosa: Where Your Own Grows Best
- Buds For Living
- Buddy Up to Santa Rosa
- Our Music is Better Than Your Day Job

No word yet from the city fathers of Santa Rosa.

1. I Ain't Ever Satisfied
2. Constellation Rag
3. Fair To Even Odds
4. Greenport
5. Fattening Frogs for Snakes
6. Stella Blue
7. Tell Me It's Okay

MOONALICE

At the Sonoma County Fairgrounds

6 June 2008 • Santa Rosa, California

HARMONY FESTIVAL

artwork by David Singer

678 Party Great American Music Hall, San Francisco, CA

According to Moonalice legend, one of the tribe's annual high holy days was called Burning Bud. It was a one-day event devoted to the building of a henge. The tribe was not very practical. It took surprisingly long to figure out that you can't build much of henge in one day.

The one-day limit led to much experimentation with building materials. They tried dirt. Then mud. They even tried water. They tried practically everything that was available. Then one day, someone decided to make a henge out of hemp.

They built the entire thing out of hemp and completed it in one day! It was huge!!! It smelled great!!! They wanted to call it Hemphenge. Then they set it on fire. They got really stoned. And a new name came out of nowhere. Stonedhenge.

So began the festival of Burning Bud. With it came Fire Arts and people getting buzzed and running around naked in the desert. It is our understanding that some of these customs persist to the present day.

1. Whiter Shade Of Pale
2. Fair To Even Odds
3. I Ain't Ever Satisfied
4. Crazy In Heaven
5. Wake Up Little Susie*
6. Stella Blue
7. Nick Of Time
8. Blink Of An Eye
9. Eyesight To The Blind
10. Tell Me It's Okay**

*with Lorin and Chris Rowan on guitars and vocals.
**with Mark Karan on guitar and Mookie Siegel on keyboards.

SAN FRANCISCO, CALIFORNIA
GREAT AMERICAN MUSIC HALL · OLIVE ALLEY
SATURDAY JUNE 7, 2008

FEATURING
THE BARENAKED LADIES
AND **MOONALICE**
ALSO PERFORMING
THE CRUCIBLE FIRE ARTS PERFORMERS

artwork by Claude Shade

©2008 CLAUDE SHADE & MOONALICE FM80 ARTWORK: CLAUDE SHADE   PRINTED IN THE USA

artwork by David Singer

6 • 7 • 8

BARENAKED LADIES • MOONALICE
CRUCIBLE FIRE ARTS
Roger & Ann McNamee Celebrating 25 Years
OLIVE ALLEY • SAN FRANCISCO • CALIFORNIA

artwork by Chris Shaw

6 7 8

SATURDAY · JUNE · SEVENTH

25
ANN & ROGER

BARENAKED LADIES · MOONALICE

GREAT AMERICAN MUSIC HALL

CRUCIBLE FIRE ARTS PERFORMERS

OLIVE ALLEY SF·CA

2008

MOONALICE w. BARENAKED LADIES

CRUCIBLE FIREYARD - GREATAMERICAN MUSIC HALL

25 YEARS

JUNE 27 · 28 · 08

OLIVE ALLEY, SAN FRANCISCO, CALIFORNIA

artwork by Alexandra Fischer

© STANLEY MOUSE × MM ARTWORK STANLEY MOUSE

CHRIS SHAW:

Chris Shaw was born 1967 and has been cranking out art & rock posters by the hundreds since the mid '80's. Chris creates posters using a myriad of different styles and techniques, from hand-inked illustrations, to deeply layered digital collages. Shaw is equally at ease working with classic printmaking techniques or the most current cutting-edge digital technology, and loves to combine the crafts. He has made dozens of posters for Bill Graham Presents and the Fillmore Auditorium in San Francisco, and currently works with numerous bands and venues worldwide. Chris exhibits his paintings and posters in shows and galleries in the USA and Europe and currently works from his studio in Oakland, Ca

DAVID SINGER:

David Singer is best known as one of the early Fillmore artists, designing 75 posters for Bill Graham, from 1969 to 1990. This was the era before computers changed everything in graphics. Working mostly in the medium of collage, he has now switched from analog cut-and-paste methods to total digital manipulation of images. Also known for his cryptic hand-lettering, Singer designed the circular Moonalice name that appears on all his posters and is often used as a band logo. David Singer currently lives and works in Petaluma, Ca. www.davidsinger.com.

ALEXANDRA FISCHER:

A relative newcomer to the San Francisco poster scene, Alexandra Fischer brings a fresh look to the classic rock poster, working with both photography and digital collage. Often seamlessly combining her own work with found images, she creates artwork that references the colorful history of the poster while having a decidedly modern look. She has created posters for The Fillmore, Club Paradiso Amsterdam, and works with several bands and artists locally. Alex moved to the Bay Area from Germany in 2002 to study photography and film. She currently lives and works in her Oakland, Ca. studio.

STANLEY MOUSE:

The sixties, an era of untamed passion; peace, love and happiness amidst war. Somewhere between these extremities, a new style of art was born.